Relentless Pursuit

Captain F J Walker CB, DSO and three bars.

FORTUNES OF WAR

Relentless Pursuit

CAPTAIN F J WALKER, THE GREATEST HUNTER
& DESTROYER OF U-BOATS IN WWII

BY COMMANDER D E G WEMYSS

CERBERUS

First Published in 1955

PUBLISHED IN THE UNITED KINGDOM BY;

Cerberus Publishing Limited
Penn House
Leigh Woods
Bristol BS8 3PF
Tel: ++44 117 974 7175
Fax: ++44 117 973 0890
e-mail: cerberusbooks@aol.com

© Cerberus Publishing, 2003

British Library Cataloguing in Publication Data.
A catalogue record for this book is available from the British Library.

ISBN 1 84145 023 5

PRINTED AND BOUND IN GREAT BRITAIN.

Contents

AUTHOR'S INTRODUCTION
TO THE ORIGINAL EDITION

THIS story originally appeared under the rather formidable technical title of *Walker's Groups in the Western Approaches*. As such it appealed to a limited circle of readers who understood what the title meant, but for readers with a less specialised knowledge I should explain that it concerns the two Groups of ships that Captain Walker commanded, and tries to pay its tribute to a remarkable man by describing his handling of them. The new title may help to show that this is no handbook, comprehensible only by professional sailors.

The story of the Second Support Group is written from my personal experience, as I was privileged to be a member of that team and to be at sea with the Group almost throughout its career. I was not lucky enough to serve in the Thirty-sixth Escort Group as well, and so for its tale I am indebted to Captain Walker's own stories and to official accounts of the Group's actions. To round it all off, I was so fortunate as to obtain from our Commander-in-Chief, the late Admiral Sir Max Horton, the moving appreciation of Walker the man and of his influence on the successful fight against the U-boats that forms the Foreword to this book.

The Appendix, 'As Others Saw Us', is reproduced from the *Coastal Command Review* by permission of the Air Ministry and the Controller of H M Stationery Office.

Finally I acknowledge with gratitude my indebtedness to The Liverpool Daily Post and Echo Ltd. for permission to republish, to

Mrs F J Walker for placing her husband's papers at my disposal, and to my wife for her help in improving my composition.

September 1955   D E G W

Foreword

TO THE ORIGINAL EDITION
BY ADMIRAL SIR MAX HORTON

*(Commander-in-Chief, Western Approaches, from November 1942
until the command closed down at the end of the war)*

TO Frederick John Walker, whilst in command of Western Approaches Groups of anti-submarine vessels, fell the unique and signal honour of causing greater destruction among enemy submarines than was achieved by any other officer of our own or Allied navies.

I met him first in November 1942 whilst he was temporarily serving ashore in command of the Liverpool Escort Force base, obviously chafing at not being engaged more actively at sea on the job in which he had specialised. He had already won a resounding success against German U-boats and aircraft as the Commander of the Thirty-sixth Escort Group and was longing to be at close grips again at sea against them.

No one meeting him could fail to be impressed at an early stage by Walker's ardent spirit, great determination, obvious powers of leadership and great technical knowledge of anti-submarine warfare.

The opportunity to give him his heart's desire came with the advent of newly constructed escorts which were formed into the famous Second Support Group. Walker commanded this Group with outstanding ability until his death in June 1944.

His value and contribution to victory in the long-drawn-out Battle of the Atlantic was not confined to his own vessels. The new tactics he thought out for dealing with some of the more difficult problems in this fluctuating war were proved in the most practical way at sea by him and afterwards adopted for general use as standard practices in all other Groups.

He trained and welded his own Group into a splendidly efficient Band of Brothers who finally became so imbued with his methods and doctrine that they could, and did, carry out his wishes in the face of the enemy with the barest minimum of signals or use of radio telegraphy.

The spirit of emulation is a wonderful incentive and all my Groups benefited from his example and methods.

What this Battle at Sea meant to our country and allies is best expressed by our great Prime Minister of the war, Winston Churchill, when he said in 1944:

> 'We who dwell in the British Isles must celebrate with joy and thankfulness our deliverance from the mortal U-boat perils, which deliverance lighteth the year which has ended. When I look back upon the fifty-five months of this hard and obstinate war, which makes ever more exacting demands upon our life's springs of energy and contrivance, I still rate highest among the dangers we have overcome the U-boat attack on our shipping, without which we cannot live or even receive the help which our Dominions and our grand and generous American ally have sent us.'

In my opinion no single officer at sea did more than Frederick John Walker to win this battle, the hardest and longest drawn out of the war.

In conclusion let me quote a part of the epitaph I was proud to deliver at Captain Walker's impressive funeral service in Liverpool Cathedral:

> 'In our hour of need he was a doughty protector of them that sailed the seas on our behalf.
> 'His heart and his mind extended and expanded to the utmost tiring of the body, even unto death, that he might discover and

operate means for saving ships from the treacherous foe. Truly many were saved because he was not disobedient to his vision.

'Victory has been won and should be won by such as he. May there never be wanting in the realm a succession of men of like spirit and discipline, imagination and valour, humble and unafraid.

'Not dust nor the light weight of a stone, but all the sea of the Western Approaches shall be his tomb.

'His spirit returns unto God who gave it.'

CHAPTER ONE

Background

NINETEEN hundred and forty-one and nineteen hundred and forty-two were bad years in the Battle of the Atlantic. The enemy started the war with only a few U-boats, which he used in the normal manner of submerged attack by day. We lost some ships, but dealt comfortably with that scale of attack; the situation only started seriously to deteriorate when the enemy was able to increase his U-boat force and to change his tactics in attack.

Submerged attack suffers from two great handicaps. A lack of means of intercommunication makes each vessel an individual and each attack a separate operation, uncoordinated with the attacks of other submarines on the same target. A lack of speed under water hampers a submarine in moving to a position from which she can attack. The effect of low speed is less when attacking a slow-moving merchant convoy than when the target is a battle-fleet, but the Germans found the handicap so great that it led them to alter the design of their boats and their tactics when attacking.

The U-boat technique now produced consisted of control from shore in the preliminaries, and the substitution of night attacks on the surface for daylight attacks submerged. The plan that the enemy evolved was to station his U-boats as convenient and scout for the convoys with aircraft or by any other suitable means. When a convoy was located, certain U-boats were selected to make contact with it and shadow, reporting its position, its course and speed and details of its composition to the shore authorities and to the other boats that would then be ordered to attack. Thereafter the shadower, or contact-keeper, acted as a beacon to draw the attackers – the wolf packs as they were called – to the right place. When the pack had duly gathered and worked itself into a good position, the word was given and a storm broke over the convoy.

The contact-keeper was, of course, a vital link in the chain, and if the convoy escorts could find and swat him before he had drawn his pack to their intended prey it was often possible to ruin the whole of the enemy's plan and prevent the attack altogether. To do so, however, meant sending a number of the escort ships off ten, fifteen or twenty miles from the convoy on what would often prove to be wild-goose chases. If these ships missed their target they would be away from their station in the convoy screen for hours, and while they were away there was a very good chance that an attack might develop with an inadequate force left to meet it.

When an escort commander decided that he was not strong enough to afford these offensive lunges, he was to some extent on sound ground. In order to complete his attack the enemy had to come close in to the convoy, and that gave a small escort force its best chance of making contact and spoiling his aim. On the other hand the enemy was left free to manoeuvre round the convoy at will, using the U-boats' superior surface speed, which amounted to twice the speed of the normal Atlantic convoy, to attain the best attacking positions during the day and to deliver the attack and escape afterwards at night. It meant that during the day the brutes were circling within easy sighting distance, say ten to fifteen miles off, and there was nothing that could be done about it. That was humiliating and disheartening enough, often to be made worse by failure, for one reason or another, to fend off all the attackers when they came.

The remedy lay in forcing the U-boats, by some means or another, to dive and lose their mobility, and then in keeping them down until they dropped so far astern that they could be shaken off and be no longer a menace to that convoy. Better still, of course, was to sink them, so that they no longer constituted a menace to anyone, but the tale in the early days was all of shortages of escorts, and slaughtering was a luxury still only to be dreamt about. As a first step, while escorts were still scanty, aircraft provided a means of frightening the U-boats into diving without weakening the escort commander's force. The aircraft had at first to come from shore and could therefore spend only a limited time patrolling round the convoys. There were times when no aircraft could be there and there were areas in the Atlantic which no aircraft from shore could reach, yet convoys had to pass through them, and it was not difficult for the U-boat operators to work out where they were to be found. These gaps of time and place were gradually filled, first with more and better aircraft and later with the convoy's own aircraft flying from escort carriers and merchant ships. As time went on the aircraft were better and better fitted and got cleverer at sinking U-boats that they succeeded in surprising on the surface. The real solution, however, awaited the provision of more and more fast and powerful escort ships so as to go after the U-boats and slaughter them.

The background of this story of Western Approaches warfare would be incomplete without the shore command filling its proper place in the picture. At first the Plymouth command, under Admiral Sir Martyn Dunbar Naismith, embraced all the Western Approaches to the United Kingdom, but the fall of France so much increased the complexity of keeping open the western ocean supply lines that a separate command was created under Admiral Sir Percy Noble, with Commodore J M Mansfield as his chief assistant. The headquarters, together with those of No. 19 Group, Coastal Command, RAF, were set up in Derby House, a huge new block of offices in Liverpool, and the great organisation was built up that first held firm and then drove the enemy from the convoy battlefield of the Atlantic.

The first two years' work was largely improvisation. There were convoys to be brought to this country and sent out again for fresh loads. There were troops to be escorted on their way abroad – to North Africa, for example. There were supplies to be got to our people in the Mediterranean or in Iceland. The formation of the convoys and the arrangements for loading and unloading ships were not the job of Derby House, but the provision of the escorts with their duty 'to ensure the safe and timely arrival of the convoy', the fixing of routes and the ordering of diversions from those routes in the face of fresh threats of attack were all the Commander-in-Chief's responsibility. He had not only to operate the escorts at sea, but in general to organise the means of replenishing the ships, maintain them and their equipment, and give their crews spells for rest and refreshment. All this had to be done during those first two years with the slenderest of resources, in the face of the enemy's main attack at sea.

I never served in this headquarters, but I saw it at work from the 'user's' angle from the summer of 1941 onward. The staff knew all the seafarers of the command as individuals and was never too busy to listen to their tales, whether of battle and success or of frustration and mechanical trouble. It listened to suggestions and acted quickly and effectively on proposals for improvement or on complaints of shortcomings. Even in the worst times it never seemed to get rattled, but in spite of the long hours it worked in its dungeon, never by the light of day or beside an open window, it remained resolute and clear in mind and purpose. It was an organisation that inspired every confidence, and gave us at sea not only the direction but all the support that we needed.

At the end of 1942 Admiral Sir Max Horton relieved Sir Percy Noble, and soon afterwards he was joined by Commodore I A P MacIntyre as his chief of staff. This combination had already directed the submarine service in this war, and it now proceeded to build upon the foundations laid by its predecessors, the organisation for taking the offensive and sweeping on to victory in the Atlantic Battle. Increased numbers of ships and aircraft, improved equipment and new weapons were becoming available, and Derby House saw to it that all good things were used to good effect.

A tactical school, which had been set up at Liverpool by Admiral Noble, under Captain G H Roberts, with a small staff of naval officers and pensioners and a bevy of beautiful Wrens, was developed to a point where every budding commanding officer did a course in the theory of team-work among escorts, while, at the same time, fresh suggestions from escort commanders at sea were examined by means of games on the tactical board. At sea, Admiral Horton inaugurated the counterpart to this school, at which a special training team with its headquarters in Mr T O M Sopwith's former yacht, *Philante*, trained whole escort groups at a time, under their senior officers, in convoy defence operations. Our submarines used to take the place of the U-boats in these exercises, and a remarkable amount of free-for-all made the training most realistic. Eventually came the joint Anti-Submarine School, at which airmen and escort ships' officers lived together while receiving theoretical and sea training – an establishment that is still going strong.

With all this development there remained the sense of personal touch with our headquarters, at sea as well as in harbour, and by no means the least pleasant evidence of this was the personal signals we received from the Commander-in-Chief to give us the first news if we had been lucky enough to feature in an honours or promotion list.

Against this background the tales of Walker's Groups are told. In the rank of Commander, Walker commanded a close escort group in the hard times. As a Captain he commanded a support group, which was a symbol of the offensive which had been so long desired. A close escort group's first concern was for the safety of its convoy; a support group's first and only duty was to slay U-boats. Let me now introduce Walker and try to show how his Groups did their jobs.

CHAPTER TWO

THE BOSS

FREDERICK JOHN WALKER was born on 3rd June 1896, a son of Captain F M Walker, RN, and grandson of Colonel Sir George Walker of Crawfordton. He went to sea as a cadet in HMS *Cornwall* in May 1913, and was serving as a midshipman in HMS *Ajax* with the Second Battle Squadron of the Grand Fleet when the First World War broke out.

On promotion to Acting Sub-Lieutenant in January 1916, he was transferred to small ships, serving first in HMS *Mermaid* and then for nearly three years as Sub-Lieutenant and Lieutenant in HMS *Sarpedon*, a destroyer of Fifteenth Flotilla employed in screening the Grand Fleet, or in any other jobs that needed doing in the North Sea or north and west of the British Isles. His ship was based for the most part at Scapa Flow or Rosyth, and by a coincidence the squadron of the battle-fleet that she usually screened on fleet sweeps to sea contained HMS *Valiant*, in which I was serving as a midshipman.

After the war Lieutenant Walker was himself a watch-keeper in HMS *Valiant* for nearly two years, though we were not shipmates, as I had by then joined the submarine service. In January 1921 he started his technical courses preparatory to becoming one of the first specialists in anti-submarine warfare. While engaged on these courses he was detached for two months to serve in the Third Devonport Royal Fleet Reserve Battalion, which was formed to deal with the coal strike of May June 1921.

In this strange and thoroughly amusing interlude we were battalion mates in camp on Salisbury Plain – at Perham Down near Tidworth. The general idea was presumed to be that we were a reserve, ready to move into an area where there was trouble, but if that was the case, trouble never came our way. Instead we took our sailors for country rambles called route marches, mounted guards and generally played at being soldiers. We were inspected by a succession of generals, rising in importance to the GOC Southern Command himself. The officers had to put in a lot of spare-time work before they passed out in sword drill, but our elderly reserve sailors – all my section leaders were Stoker Petty Officers – were really magnificent in marching past at each inspection, though the dress rehearsals were invariably a shambles. By the end of our sojourn on the Plain we were thoroughly militarised, and the pub down the hill was stocked with Plymouth Gin, but we had to admit defeat in one particular. No amount of persuasion or threat would make our troops eat their meals in the mess-room. Their view was that as sailors they lived, ate and slept in their messes on the mess-deck, and a simple translation to any army barracks was not going to upset the habits of a lifetime in important matters like this. They might have to do a lot of strange things during working hours, but they carried their meals from the galley (or cookhouse) to their sleeping huts, and circumvented any attempt to make them eat elsewhere.

For the next eleven years Walker was on anti-submarine specialist duty, either in the Anti-Submarine School at Portland or on the staffs of senior officers. He was the Fleet Anti-Submarine Officer of the Atlantic Fleet in 1926-28, and of the Mediterranean Fleet in 1928–31. Shortly after this he was promoted to Commander, and held appointments in command of the destroyer HMS *Shikari*, which controlled by wireless the crewless battleship *Centurion* when she was acting as target for the fleet's guns, and the sloop HMS *Falmouth* on the China Station. In 1936–37 he was second-in-command of HMS *Valiant* on the Mediterranean Station, and then returned to anti-submarine work as the Experimental Commander at Portland, an appointment he was holding when the Second World War broke out. He also, during this time, reached the seniority limit for promotion; and had it not been for war service and the chance that it offered him to show his real worth, that would have been the most responsible post he would have occupied.

In January 1940 Commander Walker was appointed a Staff Officer Operations to Admiral Ramsay at Dover, and there he organised his part in the evacuation of Dunkirk, for which he was mentioned in despatches. He remained ashore at Dover until the autumn of 1941, when he was at last allowed to return to sea, and it is from this point that his career in Western Approaches starts. In October 1941 he took command of HMS *Stork* as Senior Officer of the Thirty-sixth Escort Group.

CHAPTER THREE

Thirty-Sixth Escort Group, Introduction

THE escort group that Commander Walker joined in October 1941 was typical of the close escorts of that time. It consisted of the sloops *Stork* and *Deptford* (Lt-Cdr H R White, RN) and the corvettes *Vetch* (Lt-Cdr H J Beverley, RNR), *Rhododendron* (Lt-Cdr L A Sayers, RNR), *Penstemon* (Lt-Cdr J Byron, RNR), *Gardenia* (Lt Firth, RNVR), *Convolvulus* (Lt R S Connell, RNR), *Samphire* (Lt-Cdr F T Renny, RNR), and *Marigold* (Lt J Renwick, RNR). The two sloops were the 'big' ships of the team, with the biggest armament and the best speed. They were built in peace-time and were more fully manned and better equipped than the war-time-built 'Flower' Class corvettes, and therefore the Senior Officer in charge of the Group with his staff was in one sloop, and the captain of the other was usually the officer who by seniority would act as his deputy.

It was only just before Commander Walker joined that it had become possible to form regular escort groups and to start team training. The training that had been given to ships when they were few was the best that shore authorities could devise, and had been kept up-to-date from experience gained during the war. It was necessarily hurried training and had therefore to be simply the basis on which individual captains, themselves often inexperienced as naval officers, could develop efficiency in their ships' companies. The standard obviously varied enormously, but, what was worse, co-operation between ships and co-ordinated tactics were practically non-existent when the Senior Officer met his force for the first time when they set out on the job, and many of his team were strangers to each other until they met, so to speak, on the battlefield.

It was in appreciating the possibilities that existed, now that standing escort groups were possible, and in evolving team-work tactics for his Group that Commander Walker first made his presence felt in Western Approaches. His Group was at this time engaged in escorting convoys between the United Kingdom and Gibraltar, and when they were gathered at the far end of the course, away from the distractions of home and possibilities of leave, he trained them in his own fashion. Such exercises as depth-charge loading competitions between ships improved the drill, and therefore the accuracy of firing the depth-charge patterns at sea, on which the result of attacks so much depended. He was particularly good at picking out the essential in drills or operations and making sure that performance in this respect was perfected, at the expense, most likely, of other features and regardless of what guide-books said. This training and his way of running it was a great factor in welding the individual ships into a team that looked to its Senior Officer for leadership, but felt it could rely upon each member not to let the side down.

Turning to higher tactical thought, Commander Walker evolved the first combined operation in which all the ships of his Group dealt systematically with a U-boat attack upon his convoy. It must be mentioned that most of these attacks came at night, when no one could see what was going on, and that they were so quickly over that it was of little use to wait for reports and organise counter-measures on the strength of them. The perimeter round a convoy is so long that each escort gets a big stretch to watch, and individually she can do little unless by good luck she stumbles on the attacker. Therefore a drill is necessary, and Commander

Walker's operation that he christened 'Buttercup' was designed for this purpose. It had some defects, but it proved the forerunner of a series of operations that were subsequently worked out in the tactical school at Derby House in Liverpool and passed on as drills to us at sea, the 'Fruit' operations. They became a matter of course in time, and played a big part in getting the better of the U-boat pack attacks.

After hard training the first requirement in cementing the Group's team spirit was the opportunity to put into practice in successful action what had been learnt. In Commander Walker they possessed a leader whose uncanny U-boat sense led them to their prey. By no means all the Group's voyages were productive; some were dull and enlivened only by skirmishes with enemy aircraft, alarms of threatened U-boat attacks that did not materialise, or just straight fights with the weather. The accounts of the Group's activities that follow are chosen as being typical, but do not aim to be a complete historical record.

CHAPTER FOUR

CONVOY HG 76, THE START

AT THE beginning of December 1941 there was something like a special blitzkrieg against the Gibraltar to United Kingdom convoys, with a concentration of U-boats maintained close to the westward of the Straits of Gibraltar. The Thirty-sixth Escort Group brought out a convoy from home early in the month without serious incident, but numerous attacks by local patrol ships and aircraft presaged trouble for the next homeward convoy. Its departure would, of course, be observed, and the news would get out to the waiting U-boats quite fast enough to enable them to make contact early in the voyage.

Having carried out a series of drills and competitions, the Group did a special patrol in the western approaches to the Strait with the idea of clearing the way. The patrol was hampered by the need to avoid neutral waters and achieved nothing.

On the afternoon of December 14th the convoy HG 76 left Gibraltar, escorted by the Group reinforced by no less than three destroyers, *Exmoor*, *Blankney* and *Stanley*, two sloops, *Black Swan* and *Fowey*, and the Free French corvette *La Malouine*. The destroyer *Hesperus* and the corvettes *Carnation*, *Campion* and *Coltsfoot* came and went after brief stays. For air escort purposes HG 76 had the first convoy escort carrier to see service, a converted ex-German ship taken in prize off the west coast of South America and renamed HMS *Audacity* (Commander, D W MacKendrick, RN). An extra corvette, the *Jonquil*, was attached and the opportunity was taken of this formidable escort force to slip out a tanker convoy of four ships bound for the Middle East by way of the Cape.

Matters started moving very early in the voyage with the discovery by a naval aircraft, X-812 Squadron, of a U-boat sixty miles to the northward of the convoy and steering towards it. The aircraft attacked with depth-charges as soon as the U-boat's identity had been established and made a pretty good shot at a target that was under helm while taking evasive action. No evidence was forthcoming of damage, but since the U-boat was on an attacking course when discovered and no attack materialised it is safe to say that she was put off her stroke. Commander Walker in the Stork was naturally some way from this encounter, but hearing the depth-charge explosions and seeing some calcium lights that the aircraft had dropped, he investigated, without success, and then left the *Deptford* and *Rhododendron* of his Group to continue the search for a further four hours before rejoining. They found nothing and so it must be assumed that the U-boat, though shaken, made good her escape.

Meanwhile X-812 had happened upon another U-boat on the surface, just two hours after her first sighting, but being out of depth-charges could only frown at the enemy and by looking fierce force her to dive in a hurry. This U-boat was well astern of the convoy and therefore no danger to it, and so no ships were detached to hunt.

These events proved to be just preliminary skirmishes, but the first real attack was not long delayed. Unluckily for us, it claimed a valuable victim. The tanker convoy which had sailed just after HG 76 and had kept on the south-east (or disengaged) flank during the night was attacked at 3 a.m. by a U-boat that fired two torpedoes which hit the *Empire Baracuda*. The U-boat's conning-tower was momentarily sighted from the bridge just after the explosion, and one of the escort later got a possible submarine contact on her asdic and dropped some depth-charges on it, but we must be said to have lost that round. The ship sank in about ten minutes, survivors being picked up by the corvette *Coltsfoot*, which took them back to Gibraltar. The rest of that tanker convoy went on to complete its voyage without further molestation and passes out of our story.

There was one more encounter with the enemy that night. Once again it was on the northern flank of HG 76, though well clear, and out of reach of the escort ships. A naval aircraft, B-812 Squadron, sighted a surfaced U-boat twenty-four miles south-west of Cape Trafalgar, and although the enemy dived quickly the aircraft dropped depth-charges so close ahead of the swirl and so soon after the last of the hull had disappeared that the bump must have been a good one. Damage, however, seemed to be confined to the enemy's morale, since no debris came up to gladden the pilot's eyes.

THE SINKING OF U-131

The next two days, 15th and 16th December, were quite quiet and it looked as though HG 76, having passed through a first cordon of U-boats, was moving through an empty space before entering the zone of operations off the Portuguese coast. By dusk on the 16th all the extra sloops and corvettes had left, but the destroyers *Stanley* (Lt-Cdr D B Shaw, RN), *Exmoor* (Lt-Cdr L. St G Rich, RN), and *Blankney* (Lt-Cdr P F Powlett, RN) remained. The *Audacity* was rather short of serviceable aircraft and so the few remaining were saved up for the time when it was known that there were U-boats about again. The commodore of the convoy, who was embarked in the merchant ship *Spiro*, took the opportunity of the lull to practise his convoy in manoeuvres such as altering course by wheeling and turning to evade an imaginary attack. These exercises were to bear fruit later on when an attack took place in the middle of a wheel at night, yet the manoeuvre was completed in excellent order, just as though nothing had happened.

During the night of 16th–17th December, however, indications came that a fresh lot of U-boats was closing in, and so the Audacity sent off her aircraft at dawn to have a look round. At 9.25 a.m. the aircraft reported a U-boat on the surface twenty-two miles on the port beam of the convoy, and as subsequent history shows this to have been U-131 it will be of interest to take up the tale for a bit from the enemy's side.

U-131 left the yard where she was built at Bremen in August 1941 and went to Kiel for her trials. Generally speaking, trials are not very exciting, but for U-131 there was plenty of fun. While she was engaged in a tactical exercise a Russian submarine had a shot at her with a torpedo that just missed. Next another U-boat fired a torpedo that passed directly under her, and finally she got entangled in some anti-torpedo nets, from which it took her a day and a half to get clear. In doing so she did some damage to her hydrophones which, to her ultimate undoing, was never properly repaired.

After these calamities, and about three months' more normal training she started out for war. The night before she sailed the officers held an all-night party at which much drink flowed and the captain danced a *pas seul* dressed as a woman. The following afternoon, when not far out from Kiel, she met with an accident that may well have had something to do with the party, for she came into collision with a Norwegian freighter and slightly stove in her stern. So back she went for repairs, which took a week, and on 17th November off she went again, this time without the preliminary party.

She got away without mishap and proceeded on patrol in the Atlantic. She scored a single success on a merchant ship, using six of her fourteen torpedoes to sink her, and chased two other ships, one a 12,000-ton liner, without success. By 12th December the crew were beginning to think of harbour again and expected to be ordered to Lorient in time to be home for Christmas, but these hopes were dashed when orders came to proceed to the Gibraltar area, and there was deep depression on board by the time HG 76 was sighted.

U-131 sighted HG 76 late on 16th December and directed two other U-boats to the position. That night she dived ahead of the convoy, but, due to the defects in the hydrophones, dating from the struggle in the anti-torpedo net, the captain lost touch with the situation and U-131 suddenly found herself at periscope depth in the middle of the convoy. The captain, recovering from his surprise, tried to take advantage of the situation by torpedoing something, but could not bring his torpedo tubes to bear on his chosen target on account of what he took for some snaky manoeuvres on her part. Concluding that his adversary was too clever for him, he therefore decided to pass up the chance and U-131 dived deep out of it.

At 9.25 a.m. next morning U-131 surfaced to resume contact with the convoy, but seeing the *Audacity's* aircraft she ducked down again quickly, hoping not to have been seen. We will now resume the story from our own side, pausing only from time to time to see through German eyes.

On getting the aircraft's sighting report Commander Walker set off in the *Stork* to attack the intruder, ordering his three destroyers, whose speed would get them there quickly, and the corvette *Penstemon* to steer for the spot as fast as they could go.

The destroyer *Blankney* got to the scene first, but found herself involved with false echoes on her asdic with nothing worth attacking, even for luck, before 10.45 a.m. At that time, with the *Stork* approaching, a possible contact was made and attacked, but there was no result and Commander Walker could make nothing of it. He therefore organised a search to the westward by the *Stork*, *Blankney* and *Exmoor*, in the most likely direction for the U-boat to have taken. The *Stanley* and *Penstemon* were ordered to join in as they arrived.

Meanwhile, at 10.49 a.m. the *Penstemon*, while still some way from the others, got a contact which sounded all right, and, after a thorough investigation, attacked it. The contact was lost after this, and although the *Stanley* joined in a search around, nothing further was to be found and the two ships proceeded on their way to join Commander Walker's search. In point of fact, the *Penstemon's* contact was U-131 and three of the depth-charges were very close indeed. A lot of water came in aft and the submarine, lying over at a big angle, began to sink. Oil poured into the diesel engine-room from a damaged tank and penetrated into the main propelling electric motors, though not to the point of making them unworkable.

Despite every effort to correct the trim, U-131 continued to sink. As the sea pressure increased, steel plates in her hull and bulkheads started to crack and paint peeled off them in blisters. At last there was nothing left but to blow all the tanks and try to reach the surface, and in this she succeeded with the last bit of air in the high-pressure reservoirs.

At 12.47 p.m. the *Stanley*, now in station with the searching team, beginning a sweep back towards its starting-point, sighted and reported U-131, ten miles away to the eastward. All the ships were ordered to go for her at full speed, and as the submarine still had her engines in action and commanded a good surface speed a stern chase ensued. The two 'Hunt' Class destroyers quickly drew ahead, followed by the *Stanley*, but at such long range there was not much that gunfire could do to stop her. The *Audacity's* aircraft was ordered to have a go at machine-gunning her, with the idea of delaying her through twists and turns to avoid damage, but in pressing home its attack the aircraft was shot down with the loss of its gallant pilot, Sub-Lieutenant Fletcher, RNVR. However, when the range had been reduced to seven miles fire was opened from the destroyer's bow 4-inch guns, to which the U-boat could not reply, as her only big gun was mounted on the fore side of the conning-tower. The *Exmoor*, in particular, put in some nice shooting, and when shells started falling all round, the captain of U-131 decided to give up. At 1.30 p.m. he stopped, scuttled his ship and took to the sea with his ship's company, from whence they were duly picked up.

THE SINKING OF U-434

One of the U-boats summoned to HG 76 by U-131 was U-434, and the latter was an impotent spectator of her companion's destruction. In fact the hunt for U-131 passed within three miles of her. When it was over and the ships had moved off she set out in pursuit to make contact with the convoy.

U-434 was built at Danzig and the crew thought little of the firm that built her or of the firm's workpeople, who included a number of Dutchmen. Bad defects in valve gear and machinery developed early in her war career and were never properly put right.

U-434 left Kiel at the end of October 1941, and as a first mission was sent to join a pack of U-boats lying in wait for a convoy from Halifax, Nova Scotia. Contact with this convoy was never made, and no greater success attended her efforts to take part in another pack attack near the Azores, although in this case she made contact and tried to shadow the convoy, only to lose it again.

After five weeks at sea U-434 received orders to go to Vigo, where the Germans had an organisation for replenishing stores through a merchant ship lying in the harbour. She met U-574 at sea and passed similar orders to her, which included a return to the Azores area after replenishment. The two submarines then proceeded independently northward with their crews in high good humour, since the orders to return to the Azores were, in the case of U-434, known only to the captain, and the general impression was that they were bound for Lorient with the prospect of Christmas at home.

On the way up the Portuguese coast U-434 passed close to merchant ships sailing independently, but they were small and neutral and were not attacked. On 9th December, however, off Lisbon, she made contact with the outward-bound Gibraltar convoy OG 77 and reported it, but after two wearing days of shadowing she failed to get into position to attack and finally lost the convoy altogether. The captain then thought he would lie in wait for some of our ships that he believed to be loading in Lisbon, but his crew had been without bread and potatoes for five days, and in face of their discontent he gave up this idea and went on to Vigo, arriving there very early on the morning of 14th December. Since provisioning could not be completed before daylight, U-434 lay on the bottom all day before completing the job and sailing the following night. Two days later, summoned by U-131, she was in contact with HG 76.

So far as the convoy and its escort were concerned, despite warnings of further U-boats being around, all was quiet after U-131 had been despatched. Precautions against shadowers were taken, but the night passed quietly. At 9.16 a.m. on 18th December, however, the *Stanley* sighted U-434 lurking six miles on the port quarter and the *Blankney*, *Exmoor* and *Deptford* were sent after her. The *Stanley*, of course, was also in the hunt, but her asdics had been playing tricks and could not be relied upon.

The *Stanley* was the first to approach, and when she was three miles away U-434 dived. She had in fact been lucky to be still in contact with the convoy since, as on previous occasions, the captain had lost touch at four o'clock that morning. He had then gone below after inviting the quartermaster to steer any course he liked and so it was by pure chance that at daylight he was still on the job. He dived his submarine when it was clear that he could not escape attack and fired a torpedo at the *Stanley*, which missed.

The *Stanley* with her asdic out of order could do nothing effective to attack, but she could make certain that the diving position was well marked and the enemy persuaded to remain near it. This she did by marking out a square round the spot with lines of depth-charges, and she had completed three sides of her figure and dropped nineteen single charges by the time the *Blankney* arrived on the scene.

The system worked admirably, and U-434 helped by leaving a trail of oil from some leak. Contact was very soon gained and was held by the Blankney while three quick attacks were delivered.

The charges seemed to the submarine to be raining down and to be so close as to cause damage far faster than could be repaired. The conning-tower hatch was first damaged, causing a steady flow of water into the control-room. The lights failed, the steering-gear gave out, and so badly was the vessel shaken that the stern torpedo went off of its own accord. The only remaining depth-gauge showed her to be sinking uncontrollably and within a few seconds of complete disaster the captain ordered all tanks to be blown. By this means she just managed to struggle to the surface, where she was greeted by a hail of gunfire while the *Blankney* went in to ram. That *coup de grâce* was no longer necessary, for U-434's captain had already given orders to abandon ship and she soon sank of her own accord.

TORPEDOING OF HMS *STANLEY* AND SINKING OF U-574

On completion of this operation the destroyers *Exmoor* and *Blankney*, who belonged to the Gibraltar patrol and whose fuel would not allow them to go further from their base, departed full of pride and glory, and the convoy went on without their support. This was unfortunate, as after two Focke-Wulf aircraft had appeared and been driven off by the *Audacity's* aircraft with damage to one of them another U-boat was sighted by the corvette *Penstemon* just at dusk, broad on the convoy's port bow and ten miles from it. Commander

Walker ordered the *Stanley*, the only remaining destroyer, and the corvette *Convolvulus* to help *Penstemon* chase her, but she was too fast for the corvettes, and the *Stanley* was too far off to get there before it was dark. Star shells were fired which revealed nothing, and were followed by an anti-submarine sweep by the three ships in case the U-boat had dived. Apart from the statement by the *Convolvulus* that torpedoes had been heard passing close to her, nothing was found, and in the end the hunt had to be abandoned in order to rejoin the convoy escort.

This U-boat was U-574, and in view of what was to come it was a cruel shame that she could not have been caught then. U-574 left Germany about a fortnight later than U-434 and had a very similar career. She formed part of the same pack that had no success with the Halifax convoy and later met U-434 near the Azores and got from her the orders to replenish in Vigo. She tried to attack the convoy shadowed by U434, but was driven off by the escorts without firing any torpedoes and after a couple of days gave it up. She reached Vigo first and completed her provisioning and was away again in one night. Her crew, although she had been at sea a far shorter time than her companion, suffered from the same delusion about being bound for Lorient and Christmas at home, and being a younger and more seasick lot were openly disgruntled when she turned back to the southward after replenishing. Her captain was an able officer of the sternest character who suppressed the murmurs, but despite the fresh eggs, fruit, bacon and beer that she now had on board the crew remained listless and dispirited.

U-574 was under orders to proceed to the westward of the Straits of Gibraltar when she heard and responded to U-131's summons to HG 76. She made contact and was a witness of U-131 shooting down the *Audacity's* fighter on the forenoon of 17th December, although she did not stay to see the end of her comrade's career. She was herself sighted momentarily by the *Stanley* at the same time as U-131 appeared, and drew the hunt after herself, but when the *Exmoor* and *Blankney* later made a cast in her direction she dodged them.

She seems to have followed the convoy without doing very much during the 18th December while U-434 was being sunk. At dusk she closed in towards the convoy, but was driven off as previously described. She kept touch, possibly by following her pursuers when rejoining, and closed in again from more nearly ahead in the early hours of 19th December to carry out her attack.

When she got within a few miles she submerged, but kept contact on her hydrophones. After a while the captain considered he was close enough to attack and came to the surface, only to find that he had over-done things and was in fact very close indeed to the convoy and its escorts – too close for his ship's company's nerves. However, he was not the man to waste this chance with a variety of targets to choose from and at 4.15 a.m. he fired three torpedoes from a range of 1,200 yards at the *Stanley*.

On return to her station from the pursuit at about midnight the *Stanley* was ordered to form part of the rearguard. She must have sighted U-574, for she was in the act of making her reports and indicating her exact position for Commander Walker to set his 'Buttercup' operation going when a torpedo hit her. The resultant explosion was a terrible sight, with a sheet of flame several hundred feet high, but happily there were some twenty-eight survivors, who were picked up by the *Stork* and *Samphire* some time later.

The *Stork* was also a member of the rearguard, though stationed closer to the convoy than the *Stanley* had been. She heard torpedoes that missed the *Stanley* pass astern of her as she turned to deal with the U-boat, but, bright as the illumination was from the explosion, she does not seem to have seen U-574. The German captain, on the other hand, fancied himself to have been lit up for the world to see and tried to escape at the best speed of his submarine's engines, only to have his worst fears realised by finding the *Stork* on his heels, forcing him to dive. Quick methodical action, helped by good luck, had brought the *Stork* straight to her quarry, but there was no element of luck in the establishment of good asdic contact with the submerged U-boat nine and a half minutes after the explosion.

The first depth-charge attack was delivered immediately, and was of the kind in which accuracy is to some extent sacrificed to speed when the important thing is to frighten the enemy and put him off his stroke. Unluckily the explosion of the charges upset the *Stork's* dynamo, and contact was temporarily lost until the asdic could be got working again, but within a few minutes all was well, and the U-boat, rattled by the attack, helped to give herself away by using high speed.

The next attack, though by no means deliberate, was delivered with more care, and it was dead accurate. It put U-574's electric propelling motors out of action, started an electric fire in the control-room, shattered a group of high-pressure air bottles, and started a leak in the hull. The shattering of morale was even more complete, and a violent quarrel broke out between the engineer officer, who controlled the trimming of the submarine, and his captain as to whether to surface and surrender or try to hold on.

While this discussion raged the *Stork's* ship's company was engaged in once again setting the dynamo to rights, and then in preparing a further attack. By the time she was ready the argument was settled by the engineer's ultimatum, 'Either you leave the boat or I do. I take no further responsibility.' The captain reluctantly gave the order to surface. Tanks were blown, and U-574 broke surface two hundred yards away from the Stork.

Then followed a thrilling chase. Both vessels were at full speed, with U-574 turning to port so quickly that she managed to keep inside the *Stork's* turning circle. Illumination was supplied by star shells, searchlights and snowflake rockets, but very few rounds could be got off from the *Stork's* 4-inch forward guns before they could no longer be sufficiently depressed to bear,' and she was reduced to close-range anti-aircraft weapons, small-arms fire and curses. Round and round they went as the distance apart gradually lessened, until three complete circles had been described, and then came the end. The *Stork* had her overlap and what college coxswain on the Cam or the Isis would not have sold his soul for the chance to make such a bump? Over went the helm and crash went the Stork's bow into U-574's side. The point of impact was just before the conning-tower, but where Commander Walker had the advantage over the university coxswains was in being free to bear on and roll his enemy over. She hung for a few seconds on the *Stork's* stem and then scraped on down the keel till she reached the stern, where she was greeted by a pattern of depth-charges at the shallowest settings.

A number of Germans jumped overboard during the chase, of

whom some were lucky enough to get picked up alive during the search for survivors from the *Stanley*. Neither of the principals in the underwater mutiny made any attempt to survive. The engineer officer shot himself and the captain went down with his ship.

19TH–20TH DECEMBER

Throughout these battles convoy HG 76 had ploughed steadily on unmolested, but this good luck could not hold indefinitely. U-boats had been sunk around it, but there were more of them about, and less than an hour after the *Stanley* was lost the first merchant ship suffered casualty. The officer on watch in the SS *Ruckinge*, leading the port wing column, saw a torpedo approaching his ship from the starboard bow, but it was too close to avoid and hit amidships, stopping the ship and wrecking the bridge. The ship did not sink, but lay there helpless, a target that a second shot could not miss. The crew, therefore, took to the boats to be rescued by another ship of the convoy, the SS *Finland*, and corvettes. The wreck was boarded later in the day from HMS *Samphire*, but it was decided that salvage was not practicable, and the corvette made certain of her sinking quickly by holing her with gunfire – an operation that was watched from a respectful distance by a Focke-Wulf Condor.

Soon after 11 a.m. two more Focke-Wulfs made an appearance near the convoy. These big aircraft were the scouts for the U-boat operators and were generally to be found off the Portuguese coast or in the Bay of Biscay, to the southward of the area where we kept a fighter patrol flying from shore. They either told Dönitz where we were and all about us or else they acted as beacons on which the U-boats could home. They did not expect to be disturbed except by gunfire from escorts, but this time they met opposition from the *Audacity's* fighters. One of this couple was shot down in flames and the other escaped to cloud cover, badly damaged. It was hard work for the *Audacity's* three remaining serviceable aircraft, since if much cloud was about it took two of them, one above and the other below the cloud, to deal with each Focke-Wulf. In spite of small numbers, however, they duly bagged another Fw later in the day, after such close combat that one fighter landed back on board the *Audacity* with bits of a Focke Wulf sticking to her.

In addition to beating up Focke Wulfs, the *Audacity's* aircraft scouted for U-boats, and in the afternoon of the 19th one was duly seen out on the convoy's port beam. The *Deptford*, *Marigold* and *Convolvulus* were sent out after her, but failed to make contact and, returning to their convoy stations after dark, were mistaken for U-boats by one of the escort and greeted with a firework display. In all other respects that night passed quietly.

Next morning, 10th December, the Focke-Wulf scout appeared to time, but found enough cloud to defeat even the two-fighter combination and got away. In the evening two U-boats were sighted a long way ahead of the convoy, too far off at that hour to send ships after them. The convoy made a detour around them instead and passed a second quiet night.

21ST DECEMBER
THE LOSS OF HMS *AUDACITY*

At dawn on 21st December the *Audacity* sent off an aircraft to look for U-boats and found two of them lying alongside each other with a gangplank between them. Repairs appeared to be going on in one of them and they made at first no attempt to separate or dive, but shot at the aircraft with Oerlikon guns from the conning-towers. The pilot discovered, however, that these guns did not seem to be able to elevate over seventy degrees and so he dived down from right overhead and shot three men off the plank.

After this the U-boats separated and made off, but Commander Walker, when he heard about it, felt the opportunity to bag at least the damaged one too good to miss. In case the U-boats made a fight of it on the surface with their big guns he sent a strong force of the *Deptford*, *Penstemon*, *Vetch* and *Samphire*, which, guided by the aircraft, got within twelve miles of the enemy. Then the aircraft ran short of fuel, and when the relief aircraft failed to find either U-boat the expedition came to nothing.

Two more U-boats were seen by another of the *Audacity's* hard-worked aircraft in the early afternoon, and this time the *Marigold*, which had been sent out with the *Convolvulus* after them, did get a possible contact which she attacked. This contact was further investigated, but discarded as not a submarine, and a search by the two ships revealed nothing fresh. An hour later they went on to hunt yet another U-boat that had been seen ahead of the convoy from the *Stork*'s foretop. It was clear that HG 76 was again beset, in spite of the best efforts by the *Audacity*'s aircraft and the lunges by ships in attempts to keep them at arm's length. Evasion by altering the convoy's course would not work in this case, but would simply slow down its progress homeward. It remained to try a diversion to mislead the enemy as to HG 76's real position. The *Deptford* and friends, returning from their expedition, were told to stage a mock battle of fireworks well after dark at a distance of twelve miles from the convoy, and this was most efficiently laid on. Unfortunately, however, some misguided merchant ships who also carried the snowflakes misinterpreted the affair and joined in, thus giving the show away.

The attack, when it came, was devastatingly effective. Three U-boats at least reached attacking positions at practically the same time. The first torpedoed SS *Annenone* in the centre of the rear line and sank her with only four survivors. Practically simultaneously SS *Finland* sighted a U-boat fine on her port bow and only 200 yards distant. She put her helm over, called for full speed and tried to ram, but due to lack of speed she missed by thirty feet. The U-boat slid down her side, crossed ahead of the next merchant ship in the line and disappeared, without the gallant *Finland* even being able to have another crack at her with the gun aft because the range was foul. That U-boat did no harm, but No. 3 struck us the hardest blow of all when, five minutes later she torpedoed the *Audacity*. She took some time to sink and so, happily, gave the corvettes time to pick up many of her company.

NIGHT 21ST DECEMBER: SINKING OF U-567

After the loss of the *Audacity* there were no further casualties from U-boat attacks, but the night 21st-22nd December was a grimly busy one for the 36th Escort Group. It is not easy to keep track of the numerous attacks made on U-boats during the first watch of that night, but subsequent investigations published in the White Paper on U-boat sinkings reveals, that U-567 was sunk either by HMS *Samphire* at a little after 10 p.m. or by HMS *Deptford* about two hours later. The *Samphire* never saw her target although one of the pom-pom's crew reported seeing something in the water astern soon after the charges exploded in the first attack. The *Deptford* saw her U-boat on the surface before she crash-dived and attacked her for about two hours without getting decisive results. Just when Lt-Cdr White had decided that he could not afford to be away from his convoy station any longer there came a double explosion from deep in the direction in which his asdic told him the U-boat had been. There was no further evidence of destruction and he could not tarry longer to search for it, but somewhere there U-567 disappeared without leaving any survivors.

In addition to this the *Marigold*, while going to the *Audacity*'s assistance, sighted and attacked the U-boat that had done the deed. When the *Marigold* first picked up this U-boat the enemy was zig-zagging about on the surface at high speed, and that meant at something more than the corvette's full speed. Nevertheless, a brisk chase ensued while the *Marigold* tried, and eventually succeeded, in intimidating her adversary into diving. The captain of that U-boat was a pretty cool customer, if the account of the night's work that he gave to a newspaper reporter on his return to harbour is to be believed, but he lost his nerve at the 'destroyer's' relentless pursuit. More is the pity that although 'depth-charges rained down around him' they struck his U-boat no fatal blow.

To end that first watch, the *Vetch*, while on the port beam of the convoy shortly after 11 p.m., heard a U-boat's diesel engines running fast and then suddenly dying away, as though the submarine had dived. She tried with her asdic and got contact on what proved to be a wake, but although she dropped some charges for luck the U-boat got away.

Thus ended the night's enemy activity, but there was one more incident in store for the Group's hard-worked Senior Officer. It can best be described in his own words: 'At 0517 I was aroused by an unusually ominous crash and came up to find *Deptford*'s stem about one-third of the way into the port side of my quarterdeck. The damage was serious enough, but not vital, since the main engines and the steering gear (by an inch or two) had not been touched. The after-cabin flat was wide open to the elements, but the wardroom flat and tiller flat were tight.

'I was able to go ahead again at ten knots in about ten minutes' time.'

END OF THE VOYAGE

It was upon a 36th Escort Group tired in mind and body, depleted in ammunition, and short of equipment that worked, on which the next day dawned. The crews were, however, undaunted, and the fates decided that they had had enough. HG 76 was given a peaceful day with only one attack by a Liberator aircraft on a U-boat in the vicinity. At midday a Focke-Wulf paid them a visit, circling the convoy, to be greeted by an occasional shot by the *Stork*. Towards evening two U-boats were reported by another Liberator aircraft some way off to the northward, and Commander Walker decided on another mock fireworks battle some miles away on the straight course for home while the convoy made a big diversion to one side. This time special steps were taken to see that no snowflakes would come from the convoy and the effect was all that could be desired in the way of a quiet night. Two destroyers from home joined as reinforcements on 23rd December. They put up a U-boat, which dived and made her escape while they were still eight miles off, and that was the last seen of the enemy. Shortly afterwards the *Stork* parted company for Devonport to dock for repairs, and HG 76 arrived home.

CHAPTER FIVE

THE SINKING OF U-252

ON THE night of 14th-15th April, 1942, the convoy OG 82, escorted by the 36th Escort Group, had got as far as a position 450 miles north-west of Cape Finisterre on its way from the United Kingdom to Gibraltar. There had been no remarkable incident so far, although a signal from the Admiralty warned Commander Walker that a U-boat was in his vicinity.

The screen consisted only of five ships and for the night in question the corvette *Vetch* was stationed ahead of the whole cavalcade to act as a scout. The corvette *Penstemon* was in the normal ahead screening position, the corvettes *Convolvulus* and *Gardenia* were to port and starboard of the convoy respectively, and Commander Walker in the *Stork* was in his usual place astern. This, incidentally, was the *Stork*'s first trip after the repair of all the damage she received from friend and foe in escorting HG 76. The course of the convoy was south-south-east and the speed about the usual eight knots.

The ships on the screen were, as usual, carrying out wide independent zig-zags, which had brought the *Vetch* ahead of the left-hand column of the convoy, when at 9.45 p.m. she detected an object to the north-eastward and closed to investigate it. About twelve minutes later her captain, Lt-Cdr H J Beverley, RNR, had very nearly come to the conclusion that the dark shape he saw was his colleague the *Penstemon*, bows on to him, but at the same time there was a doubt in his mind. The *Penstemon* ought not to be so far over to port as this vessel was, and although it was quite possibly a false alarm, he decided to clear up the matter of her identity and ordered star shell to be fired. The illumination justified his doubts, for it revealed a U-boat on the surface, a little over a mile away, steering a course directly towards the convoy.

The reactions of both ships, were immediate. The U-boat turned and fired both her stern torpedo tubes at the *Vetch*, which missed, the torpedoes passing down the port side twenty to thirty feet away. Simultaneously, the *Vetch* opened fire with her one 4-inch gun and shot with sufficient accuracy to deflect the U-boat's captain from his attack into seeking safety in flight. Both vessels were now going as fast as they could on courses between north and north-east, away from the convoy.

The first thing that Commander Walker knew about all this was when he saw the star shell bursting apparently on the convoy's port beam. He had no report of an enemy having been sighted because, in the heat of battle, the *Vetch* had rather excusably omitted to say anything. His first enquiry as to what was up was therefore addressed to the *Convolvulus*, the ship whose station was to port of the convoy, but the *Vetch*, hearing this and realising that his silence was causing confusion, made his report and showed where the enemy now was by directing a stream of tracer bullets at her. That explained the position, and Commander Walker ordered the *Penstemon*, *Gardenia* and *Convolvulus* to stay with the convoy while he joined the *Vetch* in the chase.

For the next half-hour the situation remained, almost unchanged. The *Vetch*'s best speed hardly enabled her to gain at all on the U-boat, although she managed to maintain a position on her starboard quarter at a range of about a mile. From here she was able to profit by the star-shell illumination put up by the *Stork* from a position three miles astern to keep up a hot fire with a variety of weapons, 4-inch, Oerlikon and Lewis guns, which kept the U-boat edging away to port and helped the *Stork* to catch up by cutting corners. The *Stork* had four 4-inch guns forward and so was able to supplement her consort's gunfire, besides providing the illumination, and a slightly higher full-speed enabled her very gradually to creep up. She was still, however, nearly one and a half miles away and on the point of running out of star shell when U-252's captain decided he had had enough and dived at 10.39 p.m.

The slight decrease of speed which accompanied the act of diving enabled the *Vetch* to be only half a mile away when U-252 disappeared and Lt-Cdr Beverley lost no time in continuing the attack with his depth-charges. The first pattern was exploding about the enemy only three minutes after she dived and although they were not close enough to do any material harm, they dispelled any illusion of an escape to safety that U-252's crew may have had.

The *Stork* gained contact on asdic very soon, but took more time to study the situation before delivering her attack. The result, ten minutes later, was described by Commander, Walker as 'no perfect drill-book attack' but it was, nevertheless, sufficiently accurate to be going on with. After it U-252 reduced her speed to dead slow, and never increased it again, though there is nothing to show whether this was enforced by damage or whether her captain hoped by this means to keep quiet and slip away.

The next attack, delivered, by the *Stork* six minutes later, undoubtedly did severe damage, although at the time it was thought the enemy had changed depth at the last minute so that the charges had gone off beneath her. Commander Walker had drawn off while reloading and was preparing with great deliberation to repeat the dose when his asdic experts, Lieutenant Impey, Leading Seaman Kelly and the rest, reported that they could hear the unmistakable sound of U-252 blowing tanks. This meant that the submarine must be in difficulty with her trim to take such drastic measures to stop herself from sinking and that this was probably an attempt to get her up to the surface.

When nothing appeared, however, Commander Walker went on with his attack, and this one U-252 took where the chicken took the axe. The *Vetch*, who had been hanging round longing to have another go, then took her chance and her charges broke up what remained of the enemy. After that neither ship could get any more contact on asdic.

Northing was to be left to chance, however, and so after firing off a few remaining star shell and finding nothing, the *Stork* did a short search in a north-westerly direction, which was the enemy's last observed course. The *Vetch* was also ordered to search around and it was half an hour before the two ships got back to the scene of the last attack to have another look for evidence.

This time the *Stork* let off snowflake rockets, which gave a fine bright illumination of the water close to the ship and straight away found what everyone was looking for. There was still a risk of another U-boat being about to take a shot at any sitting target and so the *Vetch* was ordered to patrol in a circle round the *Stork* while the latter lowered her boat to collect evidence.

Of debris there was plenty and the boat's crew could take their choice. They found a look-out's sheep-skin coat, with leather trousers, in the pocket of which was a strip of paper with the number of the U-boat on it. There were locker lids, pieces of furniture, clothing and chunks of a black cork-like substance used for lagging the bulkheads. There were human remains that made the boat's crew squeamish about touching them, but yet no complete corpse that could be given a decent burial. There was little time to spend, once the claim to have sunk U-252 had been established without doubt, and when that had been done the *Stork* re-hoisted her boat and the two ships set off after the convoy. It took them nearly four hours to regain their station.

This engagement is a pretty example of a Walker group in action. There is the leader's quick appreciation of what has happened on which he decides to hunt to death; he divides the group into hunting force and continuing escort force and with very little information and only the smallest excess of speed joins up with a hunt that is passing him in the dark at over twenty-five miles an hour and takes the position where his ship can do the most good. There is the excellent team-work of the two ships, the *Stork* and the *Vetch*, in carrying out their separate duties in the hunt with the minimum of orders as to how each ship is to act. There is the remorseless skill of Commander Walker and his asdic and depth-charge teams in destroying the enemy when once he has been driven under water. There is that excellence of drill at the guns, at the depth-charge

Chutes and throwers, in the instrument-rooms, in the engine- and boiler-rooms that is required to produce continual illumination of the tiny dodging target and a rapid succession of accurate depth-charge attacks at night. Finally, there is the Senior Officer's typical account, on which this tale is based, in which the lion's share of the credit is given to his team.

CHAPTER SIX

CONVOY HG 84

THE two previous tales have been success stories with trophies and prisoners of war, the subjects of praise and congratulation. It may seem to some readers that a good and efficient Group, such as Commander Walker commanded, needed only the presence of the enemy to move from one U-boat sinking to the next while less successful Groups were left to do the straight slogging without result. A tendency to dwell upon the successes and highlights is natural enough, while the slogging is either taken for granted or forgotten.

Here is the tale of one of the last trips that the 36th Escort Group made with a convoy from Gibraltar under Commander Walker's command, and, because it as not successful, it has proved the most difficult of the Group tales to tell.

HOW IT BEGAN

HG 84, consisting of twenty ships, left Gibraltar at 7.30 p.m. on 9th June, 1942. The escort was 36th Escort Group, reduced in numbers to the sloop *Stork* and the corvettes *Convolvulus, Gardenia* and *Marigold.* (Lt Halcrow, RNVR, had relieved Lt Renwick, RNR, in command of the latter.) As support there were present the destroyers

Wild Swan and *Beagle*, the latter only for a few hours before being detached to look for a U-boat reported to be damaged 400 miles away. A further three merchant ships joined the convoy from Lisbon at midday on 12th June, and that evening the *Wild Swan* departed for another job, leaving the *Stork* and her three corvettes as the only escort for twenty-three merchantmen. The convoy included the SS *Copeland*, a specially fitted rescue ship for picking up and looking after the crews of torpedoed ships, and one of the cargo liners, the *Empire Moon*, was fitted with a catapult from which to launch a single Hurricane fighter; this was the only provision against snooping Focke-Wulfs or bombing attack. It could only work once in each voyage, since the aircraft could not be re-embarked at sea and had either to reach a shore aerodrome before its petrol ran out or else drop into the sea where the pilot could be picked up.

The clouds began to gather for HG 84 with the sighting of the Lisbon portion by a Focke-Wulf Condor which followed the ships until they joined up with the main body and then flew round while making a full report for the benefit of the U-boat operators ashore. Commander Walker had a shot at confusing the issue by some considerable diversions of the convoy's course during the following night, but the next day, though cloudy, was clear and at 1.30 p.m. the Condor, or his brother, was in sight again.

This time it was decided to try to spoil the aircraft's report by knocking him out and so the *Empire Moon* catapulted her Hurricane without any delay. He chased the Condor for a couple of hours in and out of cloud, getting in some good bursts of fire, but finally lost him without getting the satisfaction of a kill and then pan-caked on to the sea near the *Stork*. The pilot was duly picked up and eventually returned to his ship uninjured. Unfortunately the news was out by then. Not long afterwards the U-boats were heard chattering and it soon became clear that there would be fighting that night if they, too, sighted and fixed the convoy before dark.

There were two alternative courses of action facing Commander Walker. On the one hand there was the active course of a lunge out in the direction of the nearest approaching U-boat, to head her off, drive her away and if possible sink her. That would be the obvious course with a strong escort force, but with only four ships the alternative of remaining concentrated so as to meet an attack with the best possible chance of beating it off near its objective needed very serious consideration. A lunge into the deepfield, to be effective, meant despatching half the force and it would be away for many hours because the ships were corvettes with low speed and not fast ships like destroyers. In its absence the screen around the convoy would be full of holes through which their U-boat, if the striking force missed her, and any others could approach without interference. There was also the moral effect on the merchant ships to be considered when they saw themselves almost denuded of their escort. The purpose of the escort is the safe passage of the merchant ships and they could very well argue that this point had been missed if disaster followed the despatch of a large part of the escort on a wild-goose chase.

It was a hard decision to take but one that Commander Walker had thought out in advance. He chose the offensive and set out himself after the intruder, taking the *Gardenia* with him and leaving the *Marigold* and *Convolvulus* with the convoy.

NIGHT 14TH-15TH JUNE

The lunge was quickly rewarded, for within half an hour of setting out a surfaced U-boat was sighted on the horizon from the *Stork*'s foretop. Course was altered and both ships worked up to full speed with the *Stork* steadily drawing ahead of the *Gardenia*. The U-boat also turned and ran, so that for the next two and a quarter hours it was a stern chase with the *Stork* gaining desperately slowly and the *Gardenia* falling further and further behind. From time to time Commander Walker tested the range with a salvo from his forward 4-inch guns, but by 7.15 p.m. it had only fallen to a little under seven miles. Still, a gunnery engagement was being seriously considered in the hope of doing damage with a lucky shot when the U-boat captain lost his nerve and dived. Forty minutes later the *Stork* was in contact by her asdic.

During the next two hours no less than nine depth-charge attacks were made by the two ships on what proved to be a cunning and elusive enemy. At the end of that period there was no evidence of damage or destruction of the U-boat, but one of the *Gardenia*'s depth-charges had exploded prematurely and spectacularly, blowing away her ensign and doing considerable damage to machinery as well. She was seaworthy and could manage for herself, but as far as future operations with the convoy were concerned she was useless. It was now 10 p.m., and with dark coming on and the convoy a long way off Commander Walker was forced to break away in order to get back to his station before an attack on the convoy could develop. He left the *Gardenia* to sit on the U-boat until dusk, but in fact she remained in contact practically continuously until the following afternoon. From time to time Lt-Cdr Hill freshened things up with an attack until the whole of his depth-charges were expended. Finally, the U-boat went deeper and deeper until contact was lost and could not be regained. It seems fairly evident that she did not survive, but was crushed in the depths, and yet there was never any tangible evidence of destruction. Commander Walker agreed with Lt-Cdr Hill in assuming her to have sunk, and the *Gardenia* set course for home, though later she was diverted back to lend her physical presence to the escort even though she was impotent.

Meanwhile, one and a half hours after the *Stork* had started on her chase, the *Marigold* was given the bearing of another U-boat approaching the convoy from the other side. Commander Walker's doctrine being to drive off the intruder and keep him off until dark, Lt Halcrow anticipated his Senior Officer's orders and set off in chase, leaving the *Convolvulus* alone with the convoy. Again the lunge was rewarded by a sighting, and again a chase frightened the U-boat into diving. But again, alas, though contact with the submarine was gained after diving, three attacks failed to produce any visible result and when contact was then lost it was time to be off back to the convoy.

The sole remaining escort, the *Convolvulus*, was in her turn given a bearing of a third U-boat but ahead of the convoy which had to be investigated. She, too, sighted her enemy, only ten miles from the convoy, and chased her out of sight, but Lt Connell did not feel at liberty to go on any further and so returned to his station. Just before dark he made another cast in the same direction to catch his adversary if she had followed him in, but found nothing.

At nightfall matters looked promising in spite of the obvious gathering of vultures. Three U-boats had been shown what happened if they showed their faces near HG 84 and were dispersed forty-five miles to port (being sat upon by the *Gardenia* and badly shaken), thirty miles to starboard (after chase and attack by the *Marigold*), and out of sight on the starboard bow (after chase by the *Convolvulus*). The *Convolvulus* was the only escort with the convoy, but the rest of the effective force was making its way back at full speed and would be in position between midnight and 1 a.m. Commander Walker arranged with the Commodore of the convoy (Commodore H T Hudson, RNR), in the SS *Pelayo*, for a big diversion of the convoy's course to port during the dark hours.

By 1 a.m. on 15th June the three escorts were supposed to be in station, the *Convolvulus* ahead, the *Stork* astern and the *Marigold* on the starboard beam of the convoy. Actually the *Marigold* was late in getting back and was still some miles away on the starboard quarter when she was badly needed. For at that time a U-boat slipped into her firing position somewhere to starboard of the convoy, fired her torpedoes and disappeared again out into the deepfield. At 0104 three ships, the *Pelayo* (Commodore), *Etrib* and *Slemdal* were torpedoed almost simultaneously.

It was a horrid situation. Commander Walker ordered his 'Buttercup' operation, but with so few ships to respond and his own ship already low in depth-charges, it was more of a gesture than a practical step. It would have needed a very good slice of luck to have caught that U-boat and that was denied him. The convoy fired some illuminants in an endeavour to help, but simply made themselves more visible without showing up the attacker and had to be stopped doing so. No contact or sighting was made.

The rescue ship *Copeland* went to work, but with the crews of three ships in the water the job of picking them up in the dark was bound to take a long time and there was a very good chance of the *Copeland* herself getting sunk before she could catch up again with the convoy. So there was another nasty decision to be made whether to keep the escort intact round the convoy or to sacrifice a corvette to help in the rescue work and, incidentally, to screen the

Copeland until she could rejoin. Commander Walker chose the latter course and told off the *Marigold* for the job, but confessed that even after he had made the decision he was never sure that he was right. As it turned out the *Marigold* did detect a U-boat while she was picking up survivors with the *Copeland*, chased after it, illuminated it with star shell and forced it to dive. She carried out a quick depth-charge attack, but then lost asdic contact and so resumed her errand of mercy, and though that U-boat escaped, the *Copeland* with her survivors was saved by this action.

Meanwhile, the *Stork*, maintaining her guard astern of the convoy, made contact with a fresh U-boat that was coming in to attack from the starboard quarter. Closing the contact Commander Walker sighted the swirl left by a U-boat that had just dived and, gaining asdic contact, made an accurate attack with a full pattern of depth-charges. He, the expert, and all his team were fully satisfied with this attack, but he could not linger for trophies with the convoy drawing away and naked, except for the *Convolvulus*. He allowed himself the luxury of a momentary illumination of the surface of the water by firing a snowflake rocket, but then set off again for his station satisfied that if the attack by ill chance had failed to kill it had at least put paid to one U-boat's chances of attacking HG 84.

At 4.30 a.m. a second U-boat attack was delivered on the convoy. It came in all probability from the same direction as the first and claimed two victims, the SS *Thurso* and the SS *City of Oxford*. The convoy again illuminated itself and one of the ships let off bursts of tracer bullets, some of which hit another vessel in the convoy and gave her the impression that she was being attacked from the air. The *Stork* searched her area with illuminants in the hope of catching the withdrawing U-boat, but nothing came of it. The *Copeland*, again screened and assisted by the *Marigold*, picked up survivors and again the *Marigold* was called upon to deal with a U-boat. In this case it was already daylight and a Catalina aircraft which had just arrived informed her that the enemy was a couple of miles on her port bow. The *Marigold* searched an area but failed to make any contact and resumed her chase after the convoy.

To sum up the night's work, a pack of between four and eight U-boats had been encountered; the exact number of boats present cannot be determined since one or two of those driven off during the evening may have reappeared during the night and some of those encountered at night may have been there for the second time. Two attacks had succeeded, claiming five merchant-ship victims, but, as retribution, it was confidently hoped that the *Stork* had sunk one U-boat and the *Gardenia* would settle with another. The rescue of survivors from the merchant ships had been completed unhampered by the enemy and a total of 172 had been saved from the five ships, though it was deeply to be regretted that Commodore Hudson was not among their number.

15TH–16TH JUNE

Daylight on the 15th June brought welcome relief in the shape of aircraft that could do the lunges and frighten the U-boats even when they carried no depth-charges with which to attack. The aircraft were not in sufficient numbers to give a constant patrol, but they relieved the strain and only once had the *Marigold* to go out after a U-boat. She had been engaged in transferring some of the survivors picked up the night before to the *Copeland* and in doing so the two ships had dropped some way behind the main body when she sighted a U-boat on the horizon astern, following up behind. Commander Walker ordered her to drive it off and be back with the convoy by dusk, a duty she faithfully discharged. She forced the U-boat to dive after half an hour's chase and then attacked, but inconclusively. However, she steered an evasive course going back to her station, in case she was followed, and no more was heard of that intruder.

The only other incident of the day was provided by a Focke-Wulf Condor that joined the air escort for a short while at lunch-time and was warned off by a few rounds from the Stork's 4-inch. Our share in the air at the time was a Catalina which could not hope to embarrass the Condor unless he came and asked for it, and this he declined to do. After he left it was peace, but the portents were grave once more as night approached.

The situation facing Commander Walker that evening was as

follows: Of the possible eight U-boats by which he had been beset the night before two could with confidence be written off, but six might still be in a position to attack again. Patrols and sightings had established that during the day one U-boat had been ahead, one on the starboard bow and one (sighted and chased by the *Marigold*) was astern. He could not limit his liabilities to the actual sightings, because the air patrol had not been continuous throughout the day. Reports seemed to indicate a slight bias in favour of attack once more from the starboard side, but other conditions made the probable direction of attack unpredictable. He decided to place one of his corvettes on either bow of the convoy and to remain himself astern. The convoy also did an evasive wriggle in its course during the night.

In fact only one incident occurred to spoil an otherwise peaceful night. At 2.45 a.m. the *Convolvulus*, on the port bow of the convoy, sighted and illuminated a U-boat coming in to attack. She duly headed her off, forced her to dive and gave her a full pattern of depth-charges, unfortunately not very accurately delivered. The convoy then advanced upon them and contact was lost, never to be regained, although the *Stork* did her best from the rear of the convoy. A drawn battle.

16TH JUNE TILL THE END

The following forenoon, 16th June, the weather being fine and the sea calm, Commander Walker decided to replenish the *Stork*'s supply of depth-charges, which had fallen to eight, by taking some from the *Convolvulus*, who still had plenty. The first attempt was made by going alongside and passing the charges direct from one ship to the other, but the size of the swell was found to have been deceptive, and progress was so slow that the method was changed to lowering the *Stork*'s motor boat and taking the charges across in her. Even that was laborious, and when a dozen had been passed across it was decided that the ships had dropped as far behind the convoy as could be allowed and the business was given up.

A couple of Focke-Wulf Condors joined the air escort at 10.30, to be dutifully greeted by a few warning rounds of gunfire, and at noon a Catalina joined the circus, but unfortunately at half the speed of the rest. Reports showed that about five U-boats were probably still in the vicinity, but on the other hand the escort was reinforced by the return of the destroyer *Wild Swan* and the addition of the frigate *Spey* and the Polish destroyer *Krakowiak*. Therefore, at evening, when considering the plan for the night, Commander Walker decided that nothing was to be gained by evasive alterations of course and that the best thing was to go as fast as possible straight for home. This was the right answer and nothing occurred to spoil the convoy's badly needed rest.

On 17th June the *Stork*'s machinery started to give trouble after the merciless flogging to which it had been subjected. The painful disease known as condenseritis appeared and reduced the ship, except in grave emergency, to the speed of the convoy (about eight knots) on one engine. The trouble was tackled, the cause located and cured, and the engines were ready for anything again in a couple of days, due to the efforts of Mr Haddon, the engineer officer, and his men.

Dönitz, however, had not yet finished with HG 84. The U-boats had done a great deal of harm, but were not, apparently, capable of continuing destruction in the face of the reinforced escort. A new form of attack became apparent at 9.30 p.m. on 17th June, when the *Wild Swan* (Lt-Cdr C E L Sclater, RN), which had left the escort some hours previously, reported nine enemy aircraft in a position about sixty miles from HG 84 and followed that with the information that she was in danger of sinking. These bald statements covered what was a most gallant action in which this not-so-modern destroyer (our latest and best in World War I) took on an aerial horde that had set out to demolish HG 84, and knocked down something like two-thirds of them by bow-and-arrow methods before being sunk herself. Her captain survived to receive a Distinguished Service Order (DSO) in recognition of his own and his ship's company's effort.

Warnings of impending air attack kept reaching HG 84 and an aircraft sighted and reported a force of twenty enemy aircraft within easy striking distance of the convoy. The only thing to arrive, however, was the old chum, a Focke-Wulf Condor, and he turned up at the unprecedented hour of 10.20 p.m. Having broken the rule as to time, he then proceeded to break another as to distance by coming far closer than usual, a circumstance that Commander Walker seized upon to carry out a proper full-dress HA shoot, for which he had been trying in vain for months to get a target during the exercise periods at home.

With this demonstration the enemy efforts against HG 84 ended and the convoy continued unmolested to its destination. Commander Walker reported himself as proud of the offensive spirit, initiative and guts displayed by his Group, but regarded the results of this convoy as disappointing. An impending massacre had in fact been whittled down to a twenty-two per cent loss, but, as ever, he was unsparing in his criticisms of himself.

The judgement of those in high places was unmistakably shown in the next half-yearly promotions, when Commander Walker, although previously passed over, and two years beyond the promotion zone in seniority, was specially promoted to captain. Shortly after this, he temporarily left the sea to take command of the escort base in Liverpool and with his departure from it this tale of the 36th Escort Group ends. The Group went worthily on under its new Senior Officer, but at this point we part company to follow Captain Walker in his next sea command.

Preparing for convoy duty, close-escort destroyers cut through the waves.

The convoy en route.

U-boat survivors in the Bay of Biscay.

"Go on and blow his breeches off" – Captain Walker and Lieutenant Ayers, HMS Starling's navigator.

Captain Walker addressing his men.

Sir Max Horton, Commander-in-Chief, Western Approaches, with Commander Wemyss before addressing HMS Starling's ship's company on the Group's return after scoring three U-boats in a trip. August 1944.

HMS Wild Goose, taken from HMS Tracker.

British Naval officers, in a Carley float, take the surrender of U-boat.

Once the strength of the U-boats had been broken, convoys could sail the Atlantic in relative safety. Here, a British cruiser is en route to Russia in early 1945.

The armament of the two destroyers is silhouetted against the sky – their main duty is to track down submarines attacking convoys.

Britain's life-line – a convoy of merchant ships moves slowly across the North Atlantic, laden with essential materials.

Type VIIC U-boat U-333 moves quietly out of harbour to begin another long Atlantic voyage.

Navy escort ships stand by in the icy water of Hval Fjord ready to run the gauntlet again.

CHAPTER SEVEN

THE FIRST KILL

THE Group, when it was formed in April 1943, consisted of the sloops *Wren* (Lt-Cdr R M Aubrey, RN), *Woodpecker* (Lt-Cdr R E S Hugonin, RN), *Cygnet* (Lt-Cdr F B Proudfoot, RN), *Wild Goose* (Lt-Cdr D E G Wemyss, RN), *Kite* (Lt-Cdr W F Segrave, RN), and *Starling* (Captain Walker). All these ships were of the same class, the biggest and best-armed escort vessels in the Service, with good speed and endurance, and the most up-to-date anti-submarine gear of the time. The first three ships had done a few months' convoy-escort work, but the other three were straight from the builders' yards and an intensive naval work-up. The crews were very new with a considerable proportion of 'first ships,' but all the captains, and a fair number of the officers, were experienced in Western Approaches warfare.

None of us captains had served under Captain Walker before, and so we waited upon him on our first official call with no clear idea of what we were in for, except the absolute certainty that our life henceforward would not be dull.

We received at that interview an insight into our leader's character in the shape of his order book. It began with the statement that the old and familiar concern for 'the safe and timely arrival of the convoy' was to be none of our business. Our sole job was to sink U-boats and

THEREFORE… and there followed a short list of evolution's that we had got to be able to do very quickly and accurately at any time of the day or night, in any weather, and in which no sort of excuse for failure would be accepted. There followed some paragraphs in praise of the ram as 'a weapon of precision' and then a few drill manoeuvres for depth-charge attacks; in one of the drills, designed to produce a depth-charge barrage, the drastic result of failure to keep station where you could see the whites of the next ship's company's eyes while charges were being dropped, was the bumping you got when your colleague's charges went off close alongside. Finally, laid out in real detail was a scheme that he called 'Operation Haggis', for capturing a U-boat alive with all her crew, which ended with a page of useful expressions in German and Italian to hurl at the victim over the loud-hailer as an added incentive to surrender without unnecessary fuss. I think that was the sum total of his standing orders, and it is a tribute to the man that at no time did we feel in any doubt about what he expected of us, though just how we were to carry out his wishes was a matter for our common sense, and we heard from him quickly if we were wrong.

The Group set out from Londonderry a few days later, but the first patrol produced no enemy. It gave our ship's companies a chance to get over their sea-sickness, which, in my ship at any rate, was a most necessary preliminary to battle, and got us all accustomed to working together. Towards the end of May we oiled in Iceland and got down to business.

It had been established that the Germans had laid a line of U-boats about 200 miles long across the convoy route between Canada and the United Kingdom, and were employing about twenty boats on the patrol. In theory this gave so large a body of ships as an ocean convoy no chance of passing through the line unobserved, while the length of the line was too great to circumnavigate, even if its exact position was known, without spending too long on the voyage. It was decided, therefore, to accept the threat offered by these U-boats, and to send our Group through the line ahead of the convoys so as to pick up the U-boats if we could, or else to be in a good position to break up a wolf pack if we missed an enemy that subsequently sighted, and reported, a convoy.

Two or three passages through the line had been made without anything turning up, when, as we were returning to the westward to pick up an eastward-bound convoy, there came indications that a U-boat was not far away. It was on another Glorious First of June that the news came, the weather was perfect, and our leader pointed out by signal that the staff officer responsible for this clue, Lt Pitt, RNVR, rejoiced in the Christian names of Earl Howe; in fact the omens were good, We had all day to devote to the hunt, and swung into position for the chase at our best speed with hopes running high. The news travelled quickly round the ship that we were after something, and soon the bridge filled with all and sundry who felt called upon to offer advice and comment, or to seek for the latest news before dispersing to their action stations. We peered hopefully at the surface of the sea, we blessed the fine weather, for there is nothing more devastating to one's fighting spirit on an open bridge than steady rain, and we listened to the song of the asdic loud-speaker, each one keen to be the first to catch the second note of the echo which might mean contact with the enemy.

Suddenly the *Starling* turned off to starboard and slowed down. Signal flags appeared at her yard-arm to say that she was investigating a contact. She had received an echo from her asdic transmissions, but all echoes are by no means good ones of a submarine. There are many other objects that will give an echo, such as fish in shoals, or whales, wrecks or rocks on the bottom, and so on. They are lumped together under the comprehensive title of Non-subs, and have to be eliminated during the investigation before it can be said that a submarine is present. Experience is the best way of telling the difference, and the *Starling* held our most experienced men. It seemed almost incredible that this first contact, so punctually obtained, should, turn out to be the one that we were after, and yet somewhere round here we knew there was at least one U-boat. Then up went another signal, and yet another; they said that the contact was a submarine, and that the *Starling* was going to attack with depth-charges. She had 'found' and the hunt was on.

For all of us, in different ways, this hunt was something of a novelty. Those of us who had hunted U-boats while acting as close escorts had been haunted by the feeling that a convoy for which we were responsible was drawing away, possibly running into danger from another U-boat, and therefore needing the protection of a full escort. So long as the enemy being hunted was in a position to continue his attack, he was harried and never let alone, but as soon as he ceased to be an immediate menace he had to be dropped in order that the convoy escort could be resumed. On this occasion, however, time was no object. The hunting conditions were good and the day was yet young. We could afford to be as deliberate as we liked, if deliberation added to the accuracy of our attacks, and in theory there was no reason why we should not go on pegging away till doomsday, so long as we got our foe in the end.

On the other hand, having found our U-boat, we had to keep contact with her, and unless we succeeded in dealing her a lethal blow early in the hunt we should be forced to follow her every twist and turn without a sight of anything for hours on end. The risk of letting up, even for a moment, and losing contact was not one that could be accepted voluntarily, since it was odds on our losing touch altogether. The act of retaining contact, and not being led away by non-subs or by the decoys laid by a wily enemy, impose a heavy strain on the asdic team, and involve the use of only the best men. In addition we had the novelty of hunting a single U-boat with a team of six ships, and much would depend upon Captain Walker's handling of the situation if we were not to get mixed up with each other and so lose our quarry.

Early success was denied to us. The depth-charge that blows a hole in a U-boat must be correctly aimed in three-dimensions, and it is a surprising thing how close it needs to be if it is to do real harm. When the ship jumped and shuddered as a pattern went off, when it felt as if she had been hit by a great hammer, and the sea astern heaved itself up and boiled over a great area, I found myself saying: 'Well, nothing could withstand that.' Yet this U-boat seemed to thrive on it. Attack followed attack. We tried our combined attack, specially designed for just such an occasion, and the effect looked all that could be desired, yet when the commotion of the explosives had died away we looked in vain for signs of damage. There was no streak of oil leading to a bubbling source, no newly broken bits of wood or other floating debris, and our asdic told us that she was still there, moving under the water, twisting and turning.

When this sort of thing had gone on for about seven hours we lost contact. A hunt of this sort lacks much of the fine fury of battle, and contains in its place many pipes of tobacco and cups of tea, but this moment produced the nearest thing to emotion of the whole daylight struggle. In the prevailing conditions we simply could not admit that we had let our first U-boat escape to all appearances undamaged. The search around was a bit frantic, and it was with great relief that, twenty minutes later, contact was regained. The enemy, who had been ahead of the *Starling*, had made a quick turn to pass slap under her, and had almost got out of range astern before he was picked up again.

For a further four hours, until dark, the struggle went on as before. Captain Walker called us in turn to talk over the loudhailer, and in this way he kept us in touch with what was passing through his mind while he welcomed any suggestions that we had to make. It was clear that this U-boat was not only tough and well handled, but presented at least one new feature in defence that was preventing our attacks from bearing fruit. However, it was also clear that time was still on our side so long as we did not lose contact altogether. The U-boat's battery must be running down, we had heard high-pressure air being used to correct trim after some of our attacks, and air conditions inside the submarine must be deteriorating fast. This would eventually force the U-boat to surface if her crew was not to lapse into unconsciousness.

With the approach of night Captain Walker decided to cease attacking and let time and patience do the trick. He disposed us to keep the ring while he remained with the *Starling* in the middle and passed us hourly bulletins. All remained quiet, with the U-boat plodding along at about two knots and not doing anything special. Midnight approached, and we all felt that the climax was drawing near. The hunt was already the longest of the war, and if the enemy meant to try anything it would probably happen just at the time when the new watch took over for the middle watch. A few minutes after midnight it happened. A burst of gunfire and tracer came from the *Starling*, followed by the sight of a little dot in the water ahead of her in the light of her star shells and searchlights. The ships on the boundary cracked on speed and converged on the U-boat, pumping out star shells, but unable to fire anything lethal for fear of hitting each other. The *Starling*'s fire, however, was all that was necessary, and it later transpired that although the U-boat's captain had intended to beat a fighting retreat, the *Starling*'s fire had been so devastating that his gun's crew never succeeded in manning their gun. Some trouble in starting the engines completed his discomfiture, and led him to give in and scuttle the ship. For us the proceedings terminated with a signal: 'U-boat has surrendered. Cease firing.'

When we got close to the U-boat she was lying, lit up by the *Starling*'s searchlight, wallowing in the slight swell with little besides her conning tower showing. Some of her crew were to be seen on the bridge, but most of them were in the water and all were keeping up a continuous clamour, a sort of howl on a rising and falling note with no distinguishable words. The *Starling* had a couple of boats down to save life, and I was told to put down another to see if it could collect something useful in the way of secret apparatus or books. Operation Haggis should have been the next step, but could not be carried out, in spite of fine weather and a calm sea, as the nearest port was 600 miles away. I cannot say I was sorry. We had had an exhausting day, and the prospect of an immediate tow was unattractive, even when salvage and prize money depended upon it.

The U-boat settled fast, and in fact my boat, in charge of the gunner Mr G C Thompson, never got alongside her. In a few minutes her bow rose until it pointed up at an angle of about fifty degrees; she hung for a few seconds and then slid down stern first, leaving another dozen Germans in the water. Those who could do so swam over and were hauled aboard, while my boat picked up the wounded. The whole crew, except for a few men killed by the *Starling*'s gunfire, was picked up; my ship's share comprised the U-boat's captain, another officer and fifteen petty officers and men.

CHAPTER EIGHT

THE BAY, 1943

AFTER our next boiler clean at Liverpool we found ourselves taking part in a different operation. For some time Coastal Command had been building up its patrols over the Bay of Biscay to catch the U-boats on the surface whilst on passages between the Atlantic and their Biscay bases. The Germans had paid our airmen the compliment of substituting a bunch of close-range anti-aircraft guns for the single larger gun originally carried by all their North Atlantic patrol boats. When so fitted the U-boats were formed in groups of three or more for the passage across the Bay, with the idea of remaining on the surface in the face of air attack, and developing a volume of fire that would deter the aircraft from making low-level attacks. The enemy also benefited by remaining on the surface and not diving for every unidentified aircraft, since it shortened the time spent on passage, which was a period of nervous tension for those on board, yet was of no operational value.

This procedure led, at first, to heavy casualties among our airmen, and so, since escort ships were now plentiful, it was decided to intensify the struggle by bringing support groups into the Bay. The conditions that were too much for the airmen were just right for us; the U-boats were provided in concentrations miles from any helpless convoys, and we had six 4-inch guns apiece with which to outrange and batter them. When they stayed up and prepared to beat off air attack, the airmen need not risk their lives in low attacks, but could fly round out of range and whistle us up. When U-boat captains lost their nerve and started to dive, the airmen had their chance to attack while the U-boats had their trousers down, neither able to reply nor to avoid damage. If that did not succeed and we were able to get there quickly, the submarines' low speed prevented them from getting far away from their diving spot, which was accurately marked for us by the circling aircraft. It sounded all jam, so long as the weather played fair and our aircraft could avoid being driven off by the Luftwaffe.

Having lost the *Cygnet* to another Group, we set off five strong to the southward as the first Group to try this new game. We found the airmen most ready to play, and from the very beginning we were dashing hither and thither in response to sighting reports. At first we started off with a glad cry after anything that might conceivably be within our reach, but soon we learnt that discretion was necessary if all our oil was not to be burnt up in wild-goose chases. Experience taught us (I hope the airmen will forgive this) that an airman flying over the sea, at the mercy of any wind that blows, takes a larger and more broadminded view of his position in latitude and longitude than does the sailor in his crawling ship with, only the drift of puny currents for which to allow. Thus, though reluctant to give up any chance, we found it was only practicable to respond to calls that came from aircraft which said they were within thirty miles of us. When one of these came we would travel towards the scene as fast as the Group could go in a body, hoping that our ideas on navigation agreed with those of the airmen, and praying that we should arrive before they announced that they were at PLE[1] and could stay no longer.

It was on 24th June that we found our first U-boat of this series, and we came upon her by luck, not directly as the result of a sighting. We were engaged in combing an area in which a number of air sightings had been made during the last few days when the *Starling* put up her contact flags. She spent no time over an investigation, but, almost before the rest of us had realised that there was anything on, had finished her attack and the depth-charge pattern was exploding.

[1] PLE – Prudent Limit of Endurance.

There followed a sight so often featured in imaginary attacks, so hopefully dreamed of, but so very seldom seen. A few cables lengths astern of the *Starling*, and just where the turmoil of the pattern had subsided, appeared a U-boat, blown up to the surface.

The ships were spread out in a searching formation, which meant that nobody was in a position to take immediate action. There was a momentary pause while realisation dawned, and then those of us within range turned towards, cracked on full speed and opened fire. The enemy lay stopped, but was not to any appearances damaged, nor did any of her crew come out on deck. The *Starling*, being the closest, got there first, and, flashing a hasty signal to the rest of us to cease fire, went in to ram. It was a bit hard to stop our guns' crews, all of whom, of course, claimed to be hitting, and, in fact, Captain Walker informed us afterward that some friend had shot the bull-ring off the *Starling*'s bow, but the U-boat had by then regained control and was diving. The *Starling* just made it, lifting on a wave and crashing down on the hull of the submarine with her keel – an act which also opened a split in her own hull and flooded the forward magazine. She then rode on over her quarry, and the depth-charge party plainly saw the U-boat's hull under the water as it drew aft. Lt J S Filleul, RN, whose action station was in charge of this party, had been washing when the first attack was made, but flung a towel around himself and was at his post of duty in time to see another pattern of charges ready before the bump came. He thought fast and as the U-boat's hull slid under the stern fired a shallow pattern on his own initiative. That was probably the mortal blow, although the *Woodpecker* roared in as the *Starling* drew clear, and put down another rather deeper pattern to make certain. The signs of destruction came up almost at once, not in the shape of survivors, for there were none, but in broken panel woodwork, a tin of coffee, papers and so on, in the middle of a quickly spreading pool of oil. It was quickly done, and in the general rejoicing it was tacitly agreed to drop any post-mortem into who shot away the Boss's bull-ring.

After collecting evidence to convince the sceptics in London we re-formed and continued the patrol. The *Starling*'s asdic was out of action as a result of the bump, and though the leaks in her bottom were under control she was of no use without repair; and only hovered about while reports were going in for the shore people to say where she could dock. Captain Walker was still writing his report and making up his mind about the ship to which he would transfer when the next contact came. It was the *Wren* who first got contact and put in her attack, but this time there was no quick result, and 'our gallant leader' found himself impotent and a spectator.

To his great credit he did not butt in at first, but let us try our hand unaided. It was a trifle unlucky that this U-boat should have proved a tough baby, but the truth is that we did not make much of a show. For my part, I carried out two brisk attacks on what must have been decoys, and the rest of the team scratched around, gaining contact, losing it and regaining it, with no one a bit sure whether he was on a genuine submarine or a 'non-sub'. The last straw came when two of us were attacking one contact and a temporarily disengaged comrade came up with another contact a couple of miles off. His signal, 'There seems to be a second submarine here', was too much for our Boss, who, figuratively speaking, flung off his coat and sprang into the ring. He chose my ship for his flagship and, as he wanted a captain for the *Starling* he called me over. With the battle going on around us, we lowered a boat and exchanged commands.

He did the transfer properly, taking his expert team with him, and I watched him weigh in with my ship. It was pretty to watch. He went round the various contacts until he found the genuine one, that which our distant chum had called a second submarine. He pulled the team together and organised one of the 'Specials'. I forget whether it came off the first time or the second, but success was not long in coming, and by tea-time there were two U-boats in the bag. Again there were no survivors, but debris in great quantity and oil came up.

The *Starling* parted company when the result of this hunt was certain, with orders to dock at Plymouth. We had a triumphal entry into what was, most luckily, her home port, and I felt distinctly self-conscious in receiving and making suitable replies to a whole lot of congratulatory signals meant for our Boss and his ship. I felt even more embarrassed when berthing the ship, which was steering badly owing to the water she had taken in, to find a hurrah party of dockyard mates from the department I had left not long ago, all of them delighted to add bright and audible comment on my ship-handling to their cheers for the victors. However, as compensation, I was still a west-countryman by residence, and could take the fullest advantage of an unexpected bit of holiday, while my companions toiled at their eternal vigil on the seas.

CHAPTER NINE

AIR/SEA HUNTING IN THE BAY

SOME weeks went past while the Group strove in vain for further success. The airmen and other Groups struck luck, and a steady toll of U-boats was taken both in and entering the Bay, but the Second Support Group did no more than poke about and rescue some crashed airmen belonging to both sides. In an effort to help Captain Walker, Coastal Command laid on for him a daily private aircraft, and he, in his turn, suggested to the spectators in the *Starling* that it would be a nice idea if we did some flying to tell the airmen what he was about. The machine in which I did my turn was a Catalina which, the crew told me, has only one answer to a Ju 88 – to fly round inside the enemy's turning circle. If more than one Ju 88 turned up I gathered we should have had it.

We took the air at about 4 a.m. There were a couple of bunks which no one else seemed to want, and so, having got used to the idea that we were in the air, and showing no signs of falling out of it, I turned in and slept well. Later on I went up forward and sat in the nose of the machine, enjoying a lovely summer's day with mountain-tops in Spain visible at least fifty miles off. We were ordered, while on our way south, to go to the assistance of another Group that was reported to be attacking a U-boat, and the captain told me he expected to be over them a 11.15. Sure enough, at 11.05 they were in sight, and at his appointed time we were asking for orders, and how they had got on. The reply was that they had got their U-boat and only wanted a general search, but while carrying this out we sighted our own ships, and so attached ourselves to them.

I had told the airmen about the orderly manner in which our Group was accustomed to carry out its searches, and so was a bit disconcerted to find our party in no known formation, with each ship apparently playing by herself in a corner. Some patterns of depth-charges dropped, but, in fact, the Group was in an area abounding in good 'non-subs', which could only be established as such by this kind of trial and error. We prowled about round them, gazing at the surface of the sea and hoping to find a way of making ourselves useful.

Time went on and PLE had been worked out before we intercepted a signal from another aircraft of a possible sighting fifty miles away. Here was the chance we were looking for. We set off for the position and found a Liberator circling his markers, though with no sign of a U-boat or debris. Still, we had now fixed the position of the Group relative to a possible victim, and the best use of our remaining operational petrol was to bring the two together. We flew back to the Group, gave them the bearing and distance of the markers, and then spent the rest of the time flying backwards and forwards from one to the other. Before we reached PLE we had the satisfaction of knowing that the ships could see the markers, and then we set off for home. In the last of a beautiful evening we made our landfall at the Scillies and flew up-Channel to land near Poole at 10.30 p.m. As usual I felt pretty brave when it was all over, but also, as usual, I was glad when next morning the weather did not allow me to accept the airman's kind offer to return me to Plymouth by air but 'forced' me instead to go by road.

After some weeks the Group came in for a stand-easy, and Captain Walker told me that I could have my ship back. The *Kite*'s captain, Lt-Cdr Segrave, took over care of the *Starling*, Captain Walker took command of the *Kite*, and we sailed back into the Bay, where the rate of sinking U-boats was still rising.

It was 30th July that our turn came. The Group had been brought up to strength by the addition of a new sister ship, the *Woodcock* (Lt-Cdr C Gwinner, RN), in place of our missing *Starling*. We were spread out in a search line when an aircraft sighting report was picked up from quite close to the westward. This was quickly followed, as we re-formed to go to the spot, by more and more hunting cries, until it became evident that something was developing just over the horizon that involved a group of U-boats and about half a dozen of our aircraft. It was a lovely clear summer's day, and at any moment we might expect to sight the party as we drove forward in line abreast, increasing speed knot by knot in response to the *Kite*'s signals.

Sure enough, it was not long before first one aircraft and then another came into sight ahead. They were at least ten miles off, weaving patterns round a spot dead ahead of the *Kite*, and clearly attacking something, for we could pick out the depth-charge plumes and spray as the sun shone on them, though as yet the target was invisible. We were already doing the Group's full speed in formation, but that was not good enough for our leader, and up went the signal for 'General Chase'. It was a nice touch, and an unusual signal that has seldom, if ever, been used since Nelson's day.

As we closed the range it was possible to pick out one large U-boat on the surface which was going round in a circle and firing small stuff with tracer in bursts whenever an aircraft came near. The airmen did not seem to mind but were queuing up for depth-charge attacks while we came panting along, still out of range. It looked as though we should miss the whole party if this was the last survivor of the U-boat group, but she hung on, and at last we were able to open fire with our bow 4-inch. At extreme range I am sure the shooting was not very accurate, though every gun-control officer naturally claimed to have hit, and there was undoubted danger to the aircraft as they flew in low to make their attacks. However, they did not seem to mind this either, and as we were not going to stop shooting now that we had got within range the battle raged to everyone's satisfaction. What did the trick I do not know, but I suspect it was something from the air; at any rate the U-boat stopped quite suddenly, up-ended and sank.

On coming up we learnt from the airmen what had happened before we arrived. A party of three U-boats, two big ones and one smaller, had been found in company, and had formed into a ring when attacked, chasing each other round in a tight circle. One of the big ones had been hit and sunk, and when we had come into sight the smaller U-boat had dived, leaving the other big one to her own devices, with the result that we had just witnessed. Now, they said, it was up to us to find that third U-boat; they were PLE and off home, so good luck to us.

The scene of the sinking we found marked by four or five big collapsible dinghies full of Herrenfolk, the survivors from both the big U-boats. The *Kite* got a contact at once, close alongside one of the dinghies, and attacked with a depth-charge pattern. It was drastic treatment for the occupants of the dinghy, however well justified, and so it was with some relief that we saw them bob up and down in the swirling and heaving water without appearing to be any the worse for it. The contact, however, was only their own sunken U-boat, and so we spread out to search.

When you know there is a submarine about it is remarkable how many contacts appear. I had one soon after this which, from position and characteristics, seemed quite promising. I nosed round the thing, investigating, and even asked my next-door neighbour, the *Woodpecker*, to come over and see what he thought of it. It seemed good and I was just going to tell the world and attack when the Boss, who was a couple of miles away, and had been silent for some time, preceded my signal with one of his own. 'The submarine is here,' he said. '*Woodpecker* join me. Remainder patrol around us.'

Somewhat deflated, I padded round with the others and watched the favoured few in the middle. It did seem a pity and a shame, after all the fun at the beginning, to degenerate into a spectator. A couple of attacks were made and nothing much seemed to come of them, so, having passed the age when it mattered so very much what one said in signals to one's seniors, I slipped in a request to have a turn. To my surprise the request was granted, and as I turned into the centre of the ring the Boss told me to prepare for one of his 'Specials'. We moved on together, he gave the word, and in we went to the attack. The bump of the charges going off was terrific, and yet for quite a while nothing besides scum appeared on the surface of the sea. The next ship to have her turn was told off, but then … Was that just scum, or was it oil ?… What was that floating over there?… Was it there before?… Move over and take a look… Lower a boat… The debris came up gradually and was not clearly recognisable as such for some time. Then we noticed that the sea-gulls were becoming interested, and soon after that our boat's crew showed signs of excitement and appeared to have found some unusually valuable trophy: Shouts of enquiry produced no intelligible answer and so the boat was recalled. As she came alongside under the davits to hook on, the bow man held up a horrid-looking red object… 'a 'uman 'eart,' he explained.

This perfect air/sea combined operation ended with the recovery of the survivors of the two big U-boats from their dinghies, and they told us how successful we had been. The two big ones were supply U-boats proceeding to the Middle and South Atlantic where each could refuel and replenish at least eight operational boats. They had been sailing together for mutual protection against air attack, and had been given an escort of an operational U-boat while in the Bay as an extra precaution: she was the one we had got. The loss of these two supply boats would make hay of the whole U-boat campaign in their areas, and must lead to the premature recall of their prospective clients.

With this operation ended our Group's successes of the season in the Bay. We continued the patrol through August and into September, with visits to Plymouth for a stand-off, but not even the return of the *Starling* brought us any luck. We chased after U-boats all right, and on one occasion we were witnesses of a very gallant action by a Sunderland in which the aircraft carried through its attack in the face of a hot fire that killed the pilot as he sank the U-boat. The Sunderland was so badly damaged that it crashed soon afterwards and the spare depth-charges exploded, but we picked up seven of the crew apparently none the worse, as well as most of the crew of the U-boat. We did some more air/sea rescue work, and I had the satisfaction of picking up all that was left of a Liberator's crew who had been adrift in their dinghy with practically nothing to eat or drink for eight days. Of the five who got on board my ship, three survived to reach hospital ashore and to receive decorations and promotion.

However, the number of sightings decreased as the enemy found the rate of sinkings becoming too great, and reverted to submerging for passage through the Bay. More enemy long-range aircraft began to appear, some of them armed with a radio-controlled bomb that I think they had intended for bigger targets than us, but were hustled into using in an attempt to help their U-boats. Their surface craft from Bordeaux even made a trip out to our area, and as they were big destroyers with far greater speed and a heavier gun armament than we could muster we had to be circumspect in taking them on. Lastly, after a very slack spell for some months, the U-boats started to reappear in far greater numbers on the Atlantic convoy routes, armed with another of Hitler's secret weapons which became known as 'Gnat', and which was particularly intended to annoy escort vessels. It became clear, therefore, that our place was elsewhere, though it was with regret that we abandoned the warm sunshine and the calm blue seas.

CHAPTER TEN

NORTH ATLANTIC, OCTOBER-DECEMBER 1943

ON returning to the Atlantic, with winter coming on, we found ourselves chiefly occupied in fighting our oldest enemy, the weather. The idea of close air/sea co-operation in an offensive as well as a defensive way was well established, and the Americans had been having a very good time in the fine weather belt of the middle Atlantic with groups consisting of an aircraft carrier and five or six anti-submarine ships. It was thought a good idea to extend the area of such operations to the northward, and so we were given one of the Woolworth carriers, the *Tracker*, Commander D S McGrath, RN, and told to see what we could do.

The weather, as I said before, was our chief hindrance. We were working in about the longitude of the gap between the areas covered by land-based aircraft from either side, and in that part of the world the winter gales start early. I read later an official description of the operation, written in the form of a diary, which gave the impression that we had spent the whole time passing from one gale to another, though actually it did not feel as bad as that. The *Tracker's* aircraft put in a lot of flying, and we were filled with admiration at the agility and skill of those pilots in their 'stringbags'. At times they seemed literally to claw their way back on board as their landing strip dipped and heaved beneath them.

There was one particularly horrid Sunday forenoon on which four aircraft were sent off when the sea conditions were approaching the border line between 'possible' and 'unsuitable'. In my ship the wardroom cook was roasting the Sabbath joint of pork under difficulties, as not only had he to hang on for himself and field the pots and pans as the ship rolled, but he also had to manipulate a sort of torch arrangement for rekindling the galley fire, which went out if there was an extra heavy roll to port. A long swell got up that made the *Tracker* move a good deal more than our ships, and this was the state of affairs when the four aircraft returned. The first one came down, got over the deck all right and then, just as it dropped, the deck rose to meet it. Instead of touching down, it hit the deck, bounced over the arrester wires and went over the side.

We all turned towards the wreck and went on to full-speed as one man, without signal, but Captain Walker's ship got there first. The *Tracker* had stopped and tried to lower her sea boat, but she drifted so fast that she had to get clear at full-speed astern to avoid going over the spot and, incidentally, knocking down Captain Walker's mast. Happily, two of the aircraft's crew were picked up, and only one life was lost, but there were still the other three aircraft flying round to be got down on to that heaving deck. I was stationed close to the *Tracker*'s quarter, and had a close view of the subsequent manoeuvres. The second machine came down, had a lucky break, and landed safely. The next came in, but her arrival coincided with some extra big seas, and she was waved off to fly round and have another try. So it went on with endless patience and a succession of breath-holding moments of suspense until it was accomplished. One aircraft landed heavily and damaged its undercarriage, but remained on deck; the other one landed safely. On conclusion the *Tracker* thanked us for our moral support, and the patrol proceeded. We ate our Sunday pork that day with thankfulness that we had chosen the sea and not the air for our careers.

In spite of all their courage and endurance, no reward in the shape of a sighting came to the *Tracker*'s airmen, and it was chance that brought about our contact with the enemy. Since we were not much use as an offensive force if actually beset by a gale, the authorities ashore moved us about so as to avoid the worst of the weather. Thus, for a change, it was fine and reasonably calm on 6th November at a little before 4 a.m., when the *Kite*, at the starboard end of the line found a surfaced U-boat. She turned and charged, opening fire with her 4-inch guns, and having her fire returned before the U-boat dived. The snag of having a carrier with us was now evident. No sooner did a U-boat declare her presence in our immediate vicinity than a considerable part of our attacking force had to withdraw from the scene, since it would never do to leave a large, valuable and helpless ship which could take no part in the attack hanging around where she might get a torpedo into her. The *Tracker* had to be screened in case another U-boat was about, and the *Magpie*, Lt-Cdr R S Abram, RN, a new chum who had joined when the *Woodpecker* went to refit, and my ship took no further part in the proceedings.

For the next few hours silence reigned as we plodded up and down, but when news came it was decisive, if still rather scanty. The signal simply read: 'U-boat sunk. Rejoin.' I got the story from the *Woodcock* as we passed on our way to take up our station. When the *Kite*'s first attacks had not been decisive the Boss had decided that all this rushing about in the dark was a mistake, and, since the weather looked like remaining good and conditions were excellent, the best thing to do was to wait for daylight. The ships therefore went to watching stations and trailed the enemy without difficulty. In fact, when Lt-Cdr Gwinner of the *Woodcock* found himself detailed to do the first attack he felt a hunch that it must succeed, and announced to his ship's company: 'We shall be attacking at daylight and expect to sink the enemy before breakfast.' Sure enough, it was so. One of the specials was launched at 7.30 a.m. and by eight o'clock they were picking up the bits.

When we rejoined I made a signal to Captain Walker as we passed: 'Many congratulations. The *Magpie* and ourselves hope that we may play in the first eleven next time.' We then went about our daily business, which, since it was a Saturday, was to give the mess-decks an extra clean out before the captain went his rounds. I had finished my part in this routine and was just returned to the bridge when the bearing of another U-boat was reported, followed by Captain

Walker's signal to the *Kite* and *Woodcock* to look after the *Tracker* while he and his 'reserves' went off to hunt.

We ploughed on for quite some way without contact. Sandwiches appeared on the bridge for our lunch, a 'stringbag' sent by the *Tracker* to help us passed overhead, and a Canadian Liberator from Newfoundland, near the limit of his patrol, came in sight, also hoping for a show. Our enemy, however, had taken steps to avoid being sighted, and it fell to my asdic operator to pick up an echo on his instrument. Able Seaman G A F Wilkinson, the higher submarine detector, who had been hanging about ever since the chase began, slipped into the operating position the moment the contact was reported and investigated. 'Submarine' was his confident report.

The find was reported and conditions were so good that we were able to tell the Boss quite a lot about the enemy's movements, while the *Starling* was making her way over to join us. She made her contact, duly confirmed that it was 'Submarine' and announced that, since we had a good grip of the situation, she would have the first go with an ordinary attack. She went sailing in, but the U-boat must have got wind of it, for she took quick evasive action and defeated the Boss and all his experts. He announced it to the whole world at once as a thoroughly bad attack, but worse than that, the bump of the depth-charge explosions made his gyro compass turn a somersault and put his asdics out of action. He drew clear, using horrible language, and told me to keep contact at all costs, and the *Magpie* to patrol round us while he sorted himself out.

It was about an hour and a half before he had got his compass settled and announced that he was ready to take charge and do things again. During this time we had trailed the U-boat, who attempted nothing in particular and may have thought that, having shaken off the attack, she had lost us and need only keep quiet and not advertise herself to be safe. At any rate, when the *Starling* again had contact, I was told to go ahead with a Special', and all seemed set for the big blow. There was something in the air that day, though. The *Starling's* compass, which was thought to be reading right, was again found to be out; and when I ordered the pattern to be fired, Big-hearted Arthur, my usually dependable gunner, had an abberation, and fired only half the proper number of charges.

Captain Walker admitted in his report that at this juncture he threw his cap on the deck and jumped on it. I know that I engaged in a monologue into the quarter-deck telephone, with the hope that that temperamental instrument would allow Big, at the other end, to gather that he had not done well. Matters were tense indeed when, with a splash, a cylindrical object about fourteen feet long broke surface, to lie floating not far away between the two ships.

An acid signal from the Boss remarking on my manner of performing the last task set me was cut short by a jubilant: 'I am lowering my boat to recover that floating object. Join *Magpie* in patrol round me.' The appearance of the 'object' was followed by a stream of broken woodwork and other flotsam in an ever-widening pool of oil. Our look-out on patrol, I must confess, was inefficient in the extreme, since every man jack of us was trying to make out what the 'object' was. Order was not restored till the *Starling* signalled to us that she was picking up the front half of a headless torpedo, and followed that, for the second time that day, with the signal: 'U-boat sunk. *Tracker* and escort rejoin.' Bonhomie was fully restored by the last of this series of signals 'Splice the main-brace.'

The patrol thereafter reverted to a struggle against the weather, and, with fuel getting short, it was not long before we were ordered to make for Newfoundland to replenish. In getting there we ran through the worst gale of the lot, and followed it with twenty-four hours of dense fog on the Banks. We were given a warm welcome, with a brass band, by the Americans when we found our way into their base at Argentia, and a strenuous taste of their hospitality was our lot for our stay there.

We spent about a week mending weather damage and so forth, and then my ship and the *Starling* paid a week-end visit to St John for our Christmas shopping. We left the *Tracker* behind to go to the States, and the *Woodcock*, who had suffered worst from the weather, and was due for a refit anyway, went off with a convoy homeward bound. It was with our number reduced to four that we set off on the next trip.

As a first duty we had been ordered to support a convoy eastbound from Canada, but before we made contact with it we were given fresh orders and set off across the Atlantic on our own. Another convoy moving up from the Azores was known to have been located by the Focke-Wulf Condor aircraft of the German long-distance air search, and might expect to be attacked by a wolf-pack of U-boats or by Junker bombers, or both, when it got a bit further north. Our Senior Officer was told at the time at which our people at home thought the attack was likely to develop, and was ordered to be in position by then.

It meant pretty hard steaming all the way to get there, but our luck was in so far as the weather was concerned, and some three days later, just after dark, we took up our positions on the west side of the convoy with the Fourth Support Group, under Commander E H Chavasse, RN, on the east. It was a brilliant piece of staff work, for, within two hours of taking up position, the wireless chatter that presaged a pack attack started up, and we set off on our preliminary moves in the game.

I made a cast with the *Magpie* in a likely direction and was returning to my starting position when I got a report which, shorn of technicalities, amounted to: 'Don't look now, but I think we are being followed.' I felt a bit doubtful, and couldn't see a thing myself, but the report was insistent. The guns' crews were warned off, star shell for one lot and hard bricks for the others, and then the ship was turned to point her bow at the follower. The very first star shell burst right behind the target, lighting her up beautifully – it was a U-boat all right.

I think we must have got off half a dozen rounds at her before she dived, though I doubt if they did anything more than show that we were in earnest. Then, horrors. No asdic contact. We groped around, the *Magpie* and I, but not an echo could we get. It was doubtful if our U-boat had any more than a general idea where the convoy was, but our job was still to make sure that she was headed off. If her captain was a trier, he would probably surface again for more information as soon as he thought he was clear of us, and so we combed the dangerous sector with diligence.

About an hour later a burst of activity in the deep field led to my being switched to a fresh chase, and I left the *Magpie* to look for our friend alone. This was a bit of luck for my ship, since not long after starting on this mission success came at last: the asdic loud-speaker gave us a lovely echo and no doubt about this one. A quick survey of the situation showed that this U-boat was well clear of the convoy and heading away from it, giving us the chance to take time and make our attack accurate.

I passed the glad news, to the Boss, who had been chasing will-o'-the-wisps around the deep field, and was told to hang on and he would join me. By now Lt. J Evans, RNVR, my navigator, had established, almost without question, that this was our original U-boat which had made no attempt to continue on her course after diving, but had turned away to the westward and crept off. The *Magpie* therefore was told to break off her search, but to look for a fresh attacker coming in.

Our U-boat did not appear to know that we had, by pure luck, picked her up again, for she tried no kind of evasive tricks. Indeed, she broke surface again just before the *Starling* arrived, and the same gunnery performance was put up. This time I think we must have been pretty close, as she ducked down again without further ado, and we resumed the trail.

By the time the Boss had joined and got contact we were already cursed by the bogey of time, and, as if to emphasize the point, a signal came through from shore warning us to expect an air attack at daybreak. Where, in the ordinary way, we would have trailed our U-boat till it was light, we now had the uncomfortable feeling that we represented a good part of the convoy's anti-air defence, and must be back in station on the convoy in time to meet this new onslaught. We had therefore to carry on straight away with attacks, although our special methods had not been tried before in the dark.

The 'Special' was staged with great care under excellent conditions of weather and sea, and on its completion the Boss said he was prepared to stake his shirt on it having been the best he had ever directed. We waited confidently for the result, but got nothing except the unwanted echo from our asdic that told us we had missed. It was maddening, but there it was. Three more attacks produced the same lack of result. Our time limit expired and we had to go. We might have hurt her, for in the dark we could not see if there was a streak of oil coming from her, but we had not killed. We left her. There was no air attack!

The story of this night is only partly told here. The main U-boat attack developed on the other side of the convoy where the Fourth Support Group and some of the close escort had an extremely lively time. One U-boat was sunk and no attacker got off a shot at the convoy. No further attempts were made on subsequent nights, and after a while we parted company.

No long after this the Group became involved in a losing fight with the weather, and all the ships started to leak badly. It was decided that we could be spared for a bit to set ourselves right, and so, nothing loath, we returned to harbour and rounded off the year with Christmas at home.

CHAPTER ELEVEN

SIX IN ONE TRIP

THE 1944 season did not open for us until the last days of January, when the fury of an abominable month of gales had exhausted itself and the sun shone again. The composition of the Group had changed once more, for the *Wren* and *Woodpecker* had returned under new management, Lt-Cdr Aubrey having received promotion to the command of a group of his own, and Lt-Cdr Hugonin having gone ashore after a long spell of Western Approaches seafaring. The group now comprised the *Starling, Magpie, Kite, Wild Goose, Wren* (Lt-Cdr S M Woods, RNR), and *Woodpecker* (Commander H L Pryse, RNR).

On sallying forth we were given charge of a couple of carriers, HMS *Nairana* (Captain R M T Taylor, RN), and HMS *Activity* (Captain G Willoughby, RN), and, to quote our Command periodical, we had hardly taken guard at the wicket when the first incident occurred. It was 31st January in the forenoon, a lovely sunny day, and the Group was spread in a line with our two carriers zig-zagging astern of us. My ship was at the port end of the line, and I was in the chart-house talking to the navigator about his sights when we heard some commotion from the bridge, and tumbled, up to learn the cause.

It was an asdic contact, doubtful at first, but quickly changing to a 'probable submarine'. If the operator, Able Seaman W A Oldfield was right – and praise be he was a Cockney whose brain worked fast – that would place the submarine midway between my ship and the next in line, slipping quickly through the screen to get at the valuable ships behind. Where were they?... Oh, horrors! On the port leg of their zigzag, heading over my way and simply placing themselves where that U-boat wanted them for a close-range torpedo shot... He would be firing in a very few minutes now and could hardly miss.

I think that U-boat captain must have thought something like this: When first he sighted the ships of the Group, first one and then another, and made out what we were, he thought he would dodge round us, since we would be a small target for a torpedo, while retribution would be swift if he missed. Then, as more of us came into sight and he found that he was in front of our line and could not draw clear round the end of it, he said to himself: 'Well, here comes my Iron Cross,' and settled down to attack one of us. From where he fetched up I think it would be fair to guess that my ship was his chosen victim, but before he got into a firing position he took another loop round and sighted the big game. 'Iron Cross, nothing,' was his reaction, 'this means the Oak Leaves. All I have got to do is to get half-way between two ships of the screen, pointing end on to them so as to be a small asdic target, nip through the screen and the thing is in the bag. Not much fear about getting away afterwards in all the excitement. This is a piece of cake.' He crept across to his chosen point for breaking through the screen, careful not to use speed that might make him audible on hydrophones, or might show a feather from his periscope when he put that up. He kept a careful eye on my ship and my neighbour as we approached, but neither of us showed any interest. Now we were up level with him and he was just where he planned to be, half-way between us. Now he was abaft our beam, and still there was no move from us. He was safely through the screen,! No need to worry any more about us... Now, where were the big ships?... Oh, GOOD... 'Stand by all the bow tubes!'

The U-boat was abaft my beam when I started to turn towards her, and the noise of a number of ships' propellers in her hydrophones must have drowned the sound of my ship's increase of speed at the start of the attack. At any rate she made no move to get out of the way, nor did she get off her torpedoes in a hurry as I came charging in, and it looked as though the attack was unexpected up to the last moment. Then I imagine there came a cry from the U-boat's hydrophone operator of: 'Propellers... Fast... Loud... Getting Louder!' and a 'Himmel' from the captain as he swung his periscope round and caught sight of us coming. He acted fast and in time, for he dodged my pattern of depth-charges all right. His mind, however, was no longer occupied with thoughts of attacking and sinking anyone, which meant that we had achieved our first objective. His next intention, to get safely away out of all this, could be dealt with in the manner we liked best, in slow time.

My chief fear during the run-in to attack was that I should get there too late to put the enemy off his stroke. The asdic contact was grand, and the attack more or less ran itself, but try as I could to stop them those big ships would come on. Of course, the whole thing was very quickly over, though it seemed to take ages at the time, and the depth-charges produced an immediate response. With delight I saw the carriers turn and present their sterns, which meant that even if torpedoes had been fired they would now miss. With fresh heart we were now free to proceed with the second part of the programme.

There is not much more to tell. Conditions were very good indeed, and the enemy proved strangely docile after his early show of spirit. We regained our contact after the attack and had it confirmed, first by the *Magpie* and then by the Boss in the *Starling*. The *Magpie* had a go, but missed and was told to rejoin the screen. The Boss then ordered an 'Extra Special' and charges rained down. Debris and oil appeared in sufficient quantity, and that was the end of the hunt.

Ten days passed after this without further incident. We shed our big ships – without much regret, I must confess, although they had proved good bait – and roamed freely on our own. Then news that a pack attack was working up on a convoy in our neighbourhood, and we took up positions to deal with it.

The weather held wonderfully fine, and the night of 9th February was clear and moonlit. My ship was out in the deepfield on the convoy's port bow when a shout from the port lookout drew the officer of the watch's attention to a U-boat on the surface. It was a nice bit of work, as the enemy was fully a mile and a half away, with little but the conning-tower showing, and I am glad to say that the lookout, Able-Seaman J G Wall, was decorated for it.

We turned towards the U-boat at once, but before I had got to the bridge, or the guns had opened fire, she dived. The asdic team, however, did their stuff and it was not long before we had contact, had told the Boss about it, and had been ordered to hang on until he could team up as usual. The U-boat made no use of speed or violent manoeuvre to shake us off, while, since we knew that she had a long way to go before she became a danger to the convoy, we kept quiet as well. The two ships approached one another in this leisurely manner on opposite courses until it was clear that the U-boat would pass more or less directly underneath the ship. I do not suppose the U-boat realised that she had been spotted before diving, nor, apparently, did she hear anything on her hydrophones, as her next action caught us completely by surprise and made me feel extremely foolish. She put up her periscope not more than twenty yards from the ship. The lookout saw it and let out a yell: I followed his pointing arm and there it was in the moonlight, a good two feet of it. The U-boat captain evidently intended to have a good look round, and I trust he was even more surprised at what he saw than we were.

My first reaction was to go full ahead and drop a pattern: a really good shot with the port thrower would score a bull on that periscope. I had hardly got the orders to the engines, and the depth-charge party had only started to take action, when I looked in the water alongside and realised we could never make it. We might damage the U-boat, but we could certainly never get enough way on the ship to avoid blowing our own stern off. She was too close for the 4-inch guns, and the only action was the result of some quick thinking on the part of the men stationed at the close-range weapons. Ordinary Seaman R W Gates on one Oerlikon got off a pan of ammunition, and I think the stripped Lewis gun got off some rounds; at any rate tracer hopped all round that periscope, we thought we saw sparks fly from it, we hoped the fellow at the other end got an eye bath, and then it disappeared.

Having persuaded the depth-charge party not – repeat NOT – to fire, we tried to withdraw to a more convenient range to collect ourselves and continue to carry out the Boss's orders, but found that the enemy had made up his mind to beat it in exactly the same direction. We simply could not get away from him, and the situation seemed to be getting out of hand when order was restored by the arrival of the *Woodpecker*. She had been told to join in the hunt as well, and had beaten the *Starling* to it. When she had got contact there were two of us on the job and matters could proceed properly. She ran in for the first attack, dropped her charges, and the contact disappeared. Up came the *Starling*, and was directed to the spot. 'Come over here,' signalled Captain Walker to Commander Pryse, 'and look at the mess you have made.' I circled round the two of them while they established the *Woodpecker*'s success, and then we dispersed to our stations again.

That action finished at about 1 a.m. Not long after 4 a.m. I was once more flying up to the bridge to learn that Able Seaman J D Hunt, on radar watch, had detected another U-boat on the surface. The sequence of events was the same as before; she dived before we could get the guns off, we got asdic contact, told the world and were told by the Boss that he was coming. I knew, however, that this time he was a good way off and would be a couple of hours reaching me. Hang on I would, but to be stared at through a periscope twice in one night was more than anyone could stand, and so I determined to have a smack at this one right away. We might lose contact in the commotion, but we should just have to pick it up again if we missed, and, anyway, it would keep her quiet until we could attend to her properly. It worked out according to this plan. The pattern produced no evidence of damage, but we picked up the trail after our attack and followed it without trouble as the U-boat made no real effort to shake us off. The boss turned up at 6.30 a.m. and between us we put in two 'Extra Specials'. The first one winged her, and after that she left a trail of oil wherever she went; the second one got her. Again we got debris, but no survivors.

As soon as the Boss was satisfied, we were on our way again to a fresh 'incident'. From snatches of intercepted signals we gathered that the *Kite* had picked up another U-boat at about the same time as our second, which, with the *Magpie* to help, she had been hammering ever since. This enemy had proved a tougher and more wily opponent than the other two, so that all their patience and perseverance had not managed to hurt her much, although she had not succeeded in getting away and losing herself either. We sped along at a brisk pace to the scene of this struggle, a matter of thirty miles away, and on arrival I was put on patrol to keep the ring, while the Boss mixed it with the others in the middle. After all the drama of the night this was a welcome spell of quiet, though it was good to see our leader going at it with undiminished vigour. There was some hard slogging still for him to do, with this agile customer side-stepping attack after attack. The *Kite* had to be pulled out of the struggle to join me as ring-keeper because she was practically out of depth-charges. Then, at last, the end came. Our scientists ashore may not have been best pleased at the way in which it was done, but that is a technical joke not worth telling here. Sufficient to say that the *Magpie* was duly blooded, and the Group's third victim within fifteen hours was safely gathered in.

When we rejoined the convoy that evening a reshuffle was necessary. The *Starling* was practically out of depth-charges as well as the *Kite*, and so when it was clear that no more U-boats of that pack were going to have a go she went off to collect some more from a ship in another convoy. The *Kite* was ordered home and the rest of us, under the orders of Commander Pryse in the *Woodpecker*, were told to go back over the ground to see if there might be a straggler from the pack who, having failed to find this convoy, was waiting for the next one.

It was just before midnight on the following night, as we reached the end of our beat, that we 'found' again.

The moment was an awkward one, as the Group was engaged in the manoeuvre of changing the direction of search, which meant that we were not in a formation to keep clear of one another. I told the rest what I had found, and our new Senior Officer tried to confirm the contact, at first without success. Still under the influence of what I can only describe as a 'Won't be stared at through periscopes' complex, I then made to attack, and went through a hair-raising time as I had to break off and stop the ship to avoid a colleague, and then re-start the attack from only 400 yards' range. The explosion of the pattern lifted the stern of the ship, but she still held together and the instruments still worked, so the battle could proceed. Conditions for some reason were not as good as usual, and an uncomfortable time followed while we lost and regained and lost contact again while trying to follow the U-boat, which was snaking freely. The *Woodpecker* got contact firmly, though she was not sure that she had a genuine submarine echo, and only attacked it for luck, without result. Trace was then lost altogether, and it looked as though this whole operation would turn out a frost until my expert, Leading Seaman Wilkinson, and his asdic team announced a firm contact at last, well clear of consorts. It was astern and at long range, which sounded on the face of it unlikely, but Leading Seaman Wilkinson was so confident that I begged to be excused and went back after it. It got better as we got closer, until we were not only sure that we had got hold of the real thing but knew enough about it to attack. The proper form would have been to wait for a colleague to confirm, but this groping around, dot-and-carry-one business was tiring people out without getting anywhere, and so in we went. We lost contact again on the way in, but were determined to have a bang, and completed the attack. After that we waited.

There was no contact, but instead we were rewarded with sounds. First of all I was told my listeners could hear a noise as though someone was hitting a bit of metal with a hammer. That went on intermittently for some minutes, and then there followed a sharp crack: two more bangs like muffled explosions came next, and then silence.

We had heard of what the submarines call 'breaking-up noises', which come from a ship as she sinks after disappearing from view. It seemed fair to assume that what we had been listening to were breaking-up noises from a U-boat, and since other ships present had also heard them, and none of us now had a contact, it was decided not to hunt further, but to patrol around this spot until daylight and see if any evidence could be found then. We told the Boss what we had done, and gathered from his reply that he was hastening back, having replenished his stock of depth-charges, and would give us his verdict when he had seen the evidence.

The investigation at dawn was rather disappointing. There were patches of oil, of which we picked up samples for analysis, since the light diesel oil that the submarines use is different from the oil burnt in ships' boilers, and there was some wooden debris painted grey, but of a nondescript character that might have come from any kind of vessel. The Boss turned up about ten o'clock and was justifiably unconvinced, but I was so insistent with my story of the bangs that he gave us the benefit of the doubt, and decreed that we would all go back and return before dark, when he would give us his decision. We formed up and away we went. It was a long and tiresome day, and I, for one, got my head down all the afternoon to make the time pass. At 5 p.m. we were back, and what a sight met our eyes this time. An oil patch covered several square miles of sea, in the middle of which floated a convincing quantity of debris. 'The U-boat is sunk,' signalled the *Starling*. 'You may splice the main-brace.'

I think it was after this episode, and while we were drinking the King's health, that the idea of the ship's banner was born. Our Commander-in-Chief, Sir Max Horton, when he was in command of a submarine in the First World War, used to fly a black flag when returning to harbour from a successful patrol. This flag was ornamented with the skull and cross-bones and bore strange devices to commemorate exploits of which the crew was proud. The custom was widely followed in the submarine service, but, so far as we knew, had not spread to other ships. We could see no reason why it shouldn't; and if so, what class of ship could more logically adopt it than an anti-submarine vessel. Slavish copying was not called for, but something dignified as befitting to our ship's size and appearance was what we needed, and the outcome was a really handsome banner. It was dark blue in colour, with the ship's crest in white on a light-blue ground in the middle, and the devices were white. Some of these were private and have no place in this story, but the main ones, which had to do with U-boat despatches, presented something of a problem. As must be clear to anyone who has followed this history of the Group, our sinkings were nearly all of them team affairs in which it would be impossible to say whose depth-charges struck the mortal blow, and in most cases the credit for first spotting the U-boat was as great as for sinking her. How could we fairly show our ship's share? The solution came from our leader's habit of ordering the ships that he considered to have deserved their share of a kill to splice the main-brace. We therefore sewed a representation of a rum jar into the top corner of our banner for every time we had been ordered by him to splice the main-brace.

Nothing happened for a week after this, and then it became known that another pack attack was brewing, and we found ourselves attached to another convoy. Again we shared the support with another Group, so that when the attack developed, on the night of 18th February, the U-boats found strong opposition. The attack was much better timed than the last one, since the U-boats came in from different directions, and more nearly together. The fighting spirit, however, was not there, and attacks were given up as soon as a boat was intercepted. The result was a very lively night in which all but one of the attackers were caught on the boundary; the one exception, although she got to the close screen, was so harassed that eventually she went through the convoy submerged, and never got off a torpedo. Still, the result was a drawn game: no ships were hit, but neither were there any U-boats sunk.

At daybreak the convoy was clear of attack, but it was tolerably certain that the discomfited U-boats would be found not far astern of the convoy, and so that was where Captain Walker took the Group to look for them. We started the search at 9 a.m. and by 11 a.m. the *Woodpecker* had 'found'. She had plenty of depth-charges left, and so she and the *Starling* hunted while the rest of us kept the ring. It was a long hunt this time, of great interest to the people in the middle, but dull for the rest of us until the climax came. A series of attacks had damaged the U-boat until her leaks got beyond the capacity of her crew to keep submerged. She was getting heavier and heavier and. nothing further could be done, so her captain decided to abandon ship. He used the last of his high-pressure air to get to the surface, the crew got out and the submarine sank at once. We got off some shots when she broke surface, but soon realised it was a waste of ammunition and ceased fire. The whole crew was picked up.

Forming up again, we set off after the convoy, which we were told was threatened afresh, but we had not got far before we had evidence that there was another U-boat closer than that. Course was altered, speed increased, and away we went after what we fondly hoped would be No. 7 of the trip. It all seemed too easy – too easy by half.

We had had our suppers, and in each ship the bridge action teams were beginning to collect as we approached the new battleground when there came a bang. It was pitch dark and nothing was to be seen. Nothing was to be heard, either, to account for the explosion, until Commander Pryse's voice came calmly over the R-T announcing that his ship had just had her stern blown off.

That put an end to our hunt. Somehow the whole lot of us thought alike at that moment. The *Woodpecker* was our first casualty and we were going to take care of our own. We were not going to lose one of our number if we could help it, nor were we going to lose a man from her who had escaped the explosion. So that U-boat got away while we attended to our cripple.

The rest of us started an endless chain patrol while the *Starling* went alongside the wreck, found that by a miracle no one had been seriously hurt, let alone killed, and that the ship was in no danger of sinking. The weather was not so good as it had been and was getting worse, so at daylight the greater part of the crew was taken off, leaving enough volunteers to handle wires and keep things running. The *Starling* then took her in tow, though painfully slow, since with no stern and no rudder the wreck was difficult to control. We made good about a knot and a half in the right direction and the tow did not part, so hopes started to rise. They rose higher still when a tug turned up on the following day and took over the tow, bringing the speed up to five knots, and the course more directly for home. When we were ordered to turn over the escort to some frigates and make for Liverpool we felt happy that we should see our *Woodpecker* again, but it was not to be. Eight days of towing had got her almost as far as the Scilly Isles when a gale overtook her. The precaution was taken of removing everyone from the ship before dark, and it was well so. During the night she capsized and sank.

Meanwhile the rest of us, the *Starling*, *Wild Goose*, *Magpie* and *Wren*, were informed by Sir Max Horton that on our return home to Liverpool he intended that we should be cheered into harbour. And what a welcome they gave us. We steamed up the channel into the Mersey in line ahead and turned left in succession to enter the lock leading into Gladstone Dock, and there was the crowd. Rows and rows of our comrades from the escort ships were there together with the captain and ship's company of the battleship *King George V*, which was in dock nearby, masses of Wrens (who were making as much noise as all the rest put together), merchant sailors, crews from Allied ships and dock workers. To lead the cheer party stood Captain G N Brewer on a dais, himself not long returned from a career of violence at sea that included one of the longest and most savage battles fought round a convoy in the course of the whole war. He was now in command of our base, he, had strung up a hoist of flags which read: 'Johnny Walker Still Going Strong', and he conducted the cheers that greeted each of us as we took our turn to berth.

My ship was flying her banner for the first time and looked a credit to the first lieutenant (Lieutenant W P Chipman, RCNVR), and his wash-and-brush up party. My personal impressions of the proceedings, however, were overshadowed by the anxiety of having, in the midst of all this hubbub, to con the ship to her berth in the lock without hitting either the quay or the *Starling*, where the Boss was receiving his wife and daughter.

Later, when we were all berthed in the dock and had landed our prisoners, Sir Max Horton came to welcome us, bringing with him the First Lord, Mr A V Alexander, who was on a visit to Liverpool and who made us a rousing speech. The proceedings came to an end with that ever popular wind-up to a day of emotional strain, a splicing of the main-brace, which, needless to say, was duly noted on our banner, and then the lucky ones among us went on a few days' leave.

CHAPTER TWELVE

NORTH ATLANTIC – RUSSIA – THE CHANNEL, MARCH-JULY 1944

WHEN next the Group set sail our number was made up to five by the inclusion of the *Whimbrel*, a sister ship which had been trying to join up with the Group ever since its formation. She had been unsuccessful up to now because she had been out of step with her boiler-cleans, and therefore away on some other job before we were ready for service after ours. She was commanded by Lt-Cdr W J Moore, RNR, and it was our earnest hope that she would lose no time in getting blooded.

We were once more teamed up with a carrier, the *Vindex* (Capt H T T Bayliss, RN), and sent out into mid-Atlantic to roam. A general look round became narrowed down, after a week or so, into a relentless pursuit of a U-boat employed on reporting the weather, to judge by her regular signals and the small area in which she moved about. It seemed rather a pity to do away with anything so useful when weather reports were wanted just as badly by our people, working up for the Normandy landing, as by the enemy. It even seemed as if an arrangement by which the U-boat was put on trust not to indulge in any offensive action, and gave us her code in exchange for being let alone, might have avoided duplication and saved much effort and expenditure of patience. However, our doctrine was that any enemy attempt to do anything useful to his cause in our Atlantic was *verboten* and merited death, so we set to work to apply it.

That U-boat proved remarkably elusive, and at the same time we were plagued in our search for her by numbers of whales, or some kind of large black-fish, which gave good results on the asdic. In the end, however, we found her in a proper combined operation. One of the aircraft from the *Vindex* spotted her, and although she dived out of harm's way before the attack we went after her. My ship got the first contact, and the *Starling* carried out the first attack, which sank her… just like that. It may sound quixotic, but it is none the less true that Captain Walker apologised for what he described as 'my unwarrantable intrusion', since it was by now the unwritten rule that the first ship to detect had the first bang. His attack had been meant as a 'softener' or anti-periscope-starer, but turned out to have been unexpectedly accurate. It only remains to be said that the Hun, with his usual persistence, promptly replaced our victim by another weather reporter, and it was all to do again, though not by us. We were by then proceeding 'with despatch' to Scapa and wondering what it was all about, with the cook's mate strongly of the opinion that we were going to invade Norway.

The new job did not prove to be as exciting as all that, although it was an excursion into fresh fields in the shape of a Russian convoy. We gave our boilers a brush-up at Scapa and were issued with a fascinating variety of wind-proof, chill-proof, *bona fide* Eskimo clothes. We took a run ashore to admire the Home Fleet's amenities, their canteen, cinema, and Ensa shows. Some of us galloped over the moors of Hoy and marked the changes that civilisation had wrought since World War One. Most of us returned from shore thanking our lucky stars that when we stopped work and returned to harbour we usually went somewhere where there were real pubs. One of us was rash enough to say something of the sort, and had his nose bitten off for referring slightingly to our principal naval base. Then we set off for Russia.

Stirring tales have been written of the struggles round the Russian convoys, but this will not add to their number, although our outing seemed bound to be lively when we set out. The enemy had laid on a large-scale U-boat attack for the convoy before ours, which had been a flop, and there was reason to believe that Dönitz was displeased with his boys, and had told them in words of one syllable to do better next time. The German air patrols from Norway were continuous and in force, so that we could count on being spotted early in the voyage, whether out or home, which would give the U-boats plenty of time to place themselves for attack where geography makes it impossible to vary the route. Our convoy was a particularly big and valuable one and contained, in addition to the merchant ships, Uncle Sam's present to Uncle Joe of a four-funnel cruiser. A really handsome reception committee for any form of attack had been laid on, of which our Group only formed a small part, but it was felt that Captain Walker's experience would be useful, and it was a good opportunity to see what his methods would do in strange waters.

The month of April is not a bad time to make such an expedition. It is not really cold, and I found that a kapok overall on top of ordinary sea-going clothes, leather sea boots and a Russian fur cap with the ear flaps down, kept me comfortably warm by day or night, without the need for the Eskimo outfits or drosky drivers' top coats affected by the more picturesquely minded sailors. It is dark only for five hours of the night, which suited us since that is our period of greatest activity. Our airmen were, of course, correspondingly busier in the long hours of daylight, but the weather, apart from snow showers, was pretty good all through, and they made excellent use of their time.

The tale of the trip is soon told. Very early in the outward voyage the *Starling* happened on a submerged U-boat and despatched her. I do not think the U-boat had any evil intentions against our convoy, or even knew that it was there, but it is more likely that she was a new boat outward bound from Norway to the Atlantic for her first war patrol, and chiefly concerned with making a safe passage through the Rose Garden, as the Germans called an area south of Iceland where they often had a bad time. At any rate, she made no attempt to complicate Captain Walker's attack by any astute manoeuvres, and she could hardly have made a more unfortunate choice of opponent for a first trial of a keep-quiet-and-do-nothing method of self-preservation.

As the voyage proceeded a further two U-boats were put in the bag, one by HMS *Keppel* (Commander L J Tyson, RNR), the leader of another Western Approaches Group, and the other by an aircraft. Our airmen shot down half a dozen snooping aircraft, while losing one machine when landing on. That was the bag, a modest one, and the measure of our success was in defence, since not a single shot of any kind was fired at the convoy. The nights were lively while the large number of U-boats that had been duly mustered to attack us on our passage round the north of Norway tried to get in, but they did not appear to have their hearts in it, and were headed off without much trouble. We had our disappointments too, through having to leave contacts that would not yield to quick treatment, but that is the way of things when a convoy is to be guarded. The expected air attack never came, and we reached the other end punctually and complete: in fact our only straggler, when she saw the main body disappearing out of sight ahead, produced such a burst of speed that not only did she catch up again but she romped past and led the procession into harbour.

A very pleasant three days was spent at Vaenga Bay in social life with friends we had not seen for some time, while waiting for the returning convoy to muster. My Canadian first Lieutenant gave skiing exhibitions ashore, though the snow conditions could not have been very suitable since his messmates showed their admiration for his skill by pelting him with snowballs. We invested our Boss's navigator ceremoniously with the insignia of membership of the Reciprocal Club to mark his repeated attempts to mislead us in action by passing the reciprocal of enemy bearings, and before this sort of thing got tiresome we sailed on the return trip. It turned out to be a repetition of the outward one without the bag. It was, in fact, a perfect drawn game; the U-boats were there, though even less courageous than before, and only our aircraft got a sight of a single one of them. Having delivered our goods, we sewed an heraldic polar bear on our banner and returned to Liverpool to boiler clean.

The preparations for D-day in Normandy were drawing on, and the *Whimbrel* and *Magpie* were withdrawn to train for their special duties in connection with the landings. The rest of us were not in need of special training for our part in the operation, which was to be pretty much our usual job, and only the *Starling*, *Wren* and *Wild Goose* set out for the next Atlantic trip. Once again we had a carrier, our old friend HMS *Tracker*, in the party, but this time we had an added luxury in the shape of another Group whose Senior Officer was junior to Captain Walker, and which, therefore, bought at sight the task of escorting the carrier if anything happened.

For a week or so nothing came our way, and then we heard that a U-boat some 300 miles off had torpedoed an American convoy escort and had not been found. A U-boat's crew that has had a success and got away has its tail up, and is far more of a menace to peaceful shipping than before. Our Commander-in-Chief gave us his guess of the U-boat's movements after her attack, and told us to see if we could find and deal with her.

The guess was an extraordinarily good one, considering that she was in the open ocean with no restriction on the direction she might take. We got across her guessed course ahead of any practicable 'furthest on', and despite the coldness of the scent she duly turned up to answer to our asdic after three days. My ship got the first contact, and for once, when carrying out a Group hunt, the weather was not too good. The first attack was a wet and bumpy affair which did the enemy no harm, but later the weather improved as the three ships settled down to hunt. That hunt turned out to be the longest in our history, beating even our first encounter nearly a year earlier.

The reason for our failure to get our kill quickly was a technical one, discovered later after some patient research. At the time it was bothersome, but there was compensation in playing in this hunting team. By now we all knew each other so well and could appreciate the Boss's methods and act accordingly with so little trouble that we became, in the words of the official report, 'like a well-drilled three-quarter line, passing and interpassing in a way which was a pleasure to watch'. Still, this was no peacetime drill, and an obligation lay on us to produce a result, which continued to elude us throughout the day.

At nightfall we had been hunting for twelve hours, and with so small a team that meant no easing up of the strain on the asdic and plotting teams through a stand-easy on a ring-keeping patrol. There had been a prodigious expenditure of depth-charges, and we had trailed the enemy for over twenty miles, but she was alive and game, so that we might expect a kick before she gave in. She was getting exhausted, as our attacks had kept her well on the move, and so, once again, we let time take our side. We fell in astern of the enemy at a convenient contact-keeping distance, and suitably placed for a clear gun range with mutual support when she came to her last fling, and so we trailed in silence.

It was just after midnight that we noticed increased speed and movement on the enemy's part, and got a signal from the Boss: 'I think the crisis is near.' A few minutes later, there she was, on the surface and off on her engines like a mad thing, while the three of us let drive with every gun that would bear.

What followed was a thoroughly exhilarating twenty minutes. The enemy was nearly as fast as we were, and, anyway, to follow right in was to invite a torpedo from this kind of fighter. She did, in fact, fire a torpedo that passed down the *Wren's* side. As she zig-zagged we tended to get in echelon, and consort's missiles, particularly Oerlikon, went whistling and streaking past in a most suggestive way. Hits were scored on her, and one that started a fire at the after end of the conning tower gave us a fine aiming mark. Finally she altered right round and came careering straight at us. 'Here comes the last fling – she's going to ram one of us,' I thought, and besought my gunnery boys to take their time and really hit her, not that any of them listened to me for a moment. They did hit her, though, for she altered away again and slowed down; up went her bow, down went her stern and almost in one movement she slid under the water, still moving ahead slowly. There followed a muffled thud, and, a couple of minutes later, a big explosion. As she disappeared from view Captain Walker made us his first signal of the action. 'Cease firing,' it ran. 'Gosh, what a lovely battle.'

We picked up all the German survivors, but they did not include the captain or his engineer officer. The former, we learned, was killed on the bridge by shell-fire, and the latter went down with the boat while keeping his engines running. When the captain was killed the rest of the crew had jumped over the side, and so that last mad charge had, in fact, been uncontrolled. The hunt lasted altogether for fifteen and a half hours.

This proved to be the last of the Group's engagements of the season on the Atlantic convoy routes, as we were now needed to take our places for D-day. For the first time since it was formed, the Group included ships of another class in the shape of the frigates *Dominica*, *Loch Fada* and *Loch Killin*. We cleaned boilers and made good defects in Liverpool, had a brief period of exercises for the benefit of the new boys, and anchored with the rest of our force in Moelfre Bay off Anglesey, where we rode out the gale that postponed D-day by twenty-four hours. Then we steamed out and away to our starting positions.

The invasion itself was none of our business. We had got the book of words, which we were allowed to open after we had got to Moelfre Bay and were out of touch with the shore, and so we could follow the programme of what ought to be happening. For news of what was actually happening we depended upon the BBC as we waited for our own adversaries, the U-boats, to show their hand. Naturally, some days elapsed before it became clear what they were going to try, and even then, for a week or more, it was the airmen of Coastal Command who monopolised the business before the first ship success came along. We patrolled and we searched. We moved from one patrol area to another, without making contact. Our hurryings hither and thither were undoubtedly effective, since, to the miserable U-boats, the sea must have seemed full of destroying ships as was the sky of destroying aircraft, but for weeks our Group got only one clue, and then we had our eye wiped by a couple of destroyers engaged on quite another mission.

From all that hard slogging only two incidents come to mind, both of them light and of no importance. In one case, while patrolling off Brest we went quite close in to Ushant lighthouse and were challenged by flashing signal followed by 'What ship?' in English. We replied: 'Heil Hitler,' but I am afraid we had got it wrong, as the man stopped flashing, retired into his house, shut the door and refused to be drawn into any further conversation. In the other case, we were patrolling in line abreast when all of a sudden there was a bang, and a column of water shot up about half a mile ahead of us. We poked about and investigated, but could find absolutely nothing to account for it, and proceedings were terminated by our Boss signalling: 'I am afraid we must leave and put it down to an ichtheological gefuffle.'

After a month of this work we were relieved and sent home for the usual attention to our machinery. It was my ship's turn to refit, which meant we should be missing for the first time when next the Group put to sea, and it was with a heavy heart that I visited the Boss to say goodbye. I found him in very good form, after having admitted for the first time some days earlier that he was tired, which, since we had all been out of our beds for three nights in succession, had not caused much surprise. He was trying a special recording of the *Starling*'s hunting tune, and seemed completely back to normal. Yet that was the last time I was to see him, for in five days he was dead from a stroke, brought on by overwork.

The tragedy was complete, but since this is the story of the Group, I must confine myself to the Service side. Captain Walker was not only our gallant leader who had brought us, his group mates, together, had formed us into a team, and had been the inspiration of all our work. He was, by virtue of these qualities and his unique knowledge of underwater warfare, a national asset. His services had already been specially recognised by promotion after the normal time, promotion that in peace time he would never have received; he had been awarded the CB (Commander of the Bath) and four DSO's, and, lastly, from the Service he had received an unusual and signal reward in the grant of two years' extra seniority as captain. Thus he had recaptured the time he lost when 'passed over', and was well set on the way to flag rank. He was one of the very few men whom one can call irreplaceable.

His memorial remained in his work, and proper tribute was paid to his memory in a public funeral in Liverpool, and burial at sea from a Western Approaches destroyer. His Group could not be there, for they had sailed under Commander N A Duck, RNR, formerly of the *Dominica*, to carry on his work the evening before he died.

CHAPTER THIRTEEN

COASTAL WATERS, JULY 1944-MAY 1945

THE Group resumed duty in the Channel in July, but until Cherbourg was captured and the Americans swept southwards to endanger the principal U-boat bases at Lorient, Brest and St Nazaire, there was no great slaughter of U-boats by anybody. The first attempt to get into the Channel and up to their targets between the Isle of Wight and the Mulberry harbours petered out as, one after another, the boats gave up. The Snorchel, a device that enabled a submarine to charge her battery and ventilate her living spaces submerged, was not yet fitted to all the boats making the attempt, and those that had it found considerable difficulty in learning how to use it. All but a handful found the nervous strain too great, and retired into open water or returned to their bases. One crew, which had been harried particularly badly, although without damaging their boat, baled out at night, and were found floating in their dinghy by the air patrol next morning, to be picked up by the next escort ship to pass that way. The very few that reached their objective found the preparations complete for their reception, and achieved practically nothing. Still, for our Group, visible reward for work done was slow in coming.

The spell was broken on 31st July, and then in ten days we took part in the destruction of four U-boats. We were indebted in the first place for this run of success to our shore authorities for giving us the front-row seats, and moving us from place to place so as to ensure that we had every chance to find the enemy. We were indebted also, in very great measure, to the Coastal Command aircraft, and indeed the best part of the work in two cases was done by aircraft who winged the U-boats on the surface; in two cases only did we sink the U-boat by our own unaided effort. We were even given destroyers, and sometimes fighter aircraft, to keep an eye on us as we worked our way down into the Bay, where we were close enough inshore to tempt the Hun to attack us by air or surface craft. Not all our victims were at sea with any hostile intent, and indeed the survivors of the last of the four were delighted to have finished with war, and only regretted the loss of a cargo of cognac and silk stockings, which they had embarked before scrambling out of St Nazaire with the intention of taking it straight back home.

The *Starling* still led the group with the *Wren* of the old team, and the frigates *Dominica*, *Loch Killin*, *Loch Fada* and *Lochy*. It was a new chum, the *Loch Killin*, with an Australian Volunteer Reserve Captain (Lt-Cdr S Darling), who found both the first two, and alone settled the second one. She had a weapon that was new to us, and made such devastating use of it on that occasion that the U-boat came up underneath the ship and hung there for nearly five minutes, while eight of her complement, headed by the captain, climbed out on the conning tower and stepped dryshod on to her quarter-deck. It was also a case of most just retribution, since the U-boat, finding that she could not clear our search, had tried to torpedo the *Loch Killin* at close range. Two torpedoes in succession failed to run, and after that no one in the U-boat had had any clear idea of what was happening.

The third in this series went to the bottom after the air attack, and, although hit, was not too badly damaged to get to harbour. Her captain intended to wait until dark, and then make a break for it, but the aircraft flew round the spot until we reached it, and after some trouble we located the U-boat on the bottom and attacked her. There was a strong tidal stream which complicated matters, but the *Wren* put a pattern of charges close enough to do damage beyond repair, and all the crew could do was to blow her tanks and keep the submarine on the surface for long enough to bale out.

The fourth U-boat kept us chasing all night, and I am not sure that we did not start after one U-boat and finish with another. The conditions, for some reason, were abominable, and although the hunt started with the poor simpleton surfacing about five miles away, making a coloured-light identification signal, and then, not liking the look of us, diving again, we could make nothing of it. About five hours later a Sunderland saw a U-boat ten miles to the westward of us, and did a nice attack by moonlight which winged her. We moved over as fast as we could, but again got no contact until at 6.30 a.m. The fellow surfaced not far ahead of us and surrendered, scuttling the boat and taking to the dinghies. Her captain said that he also was capable of getting home, but we had been marching all round and over his head 'all night' until he could stand it no longer, and seeing us advancing again, he felt we were bound to get him this time and surrendered.

We now had over a hundred prisoners among the ships of the Group, and were told to give way to another of the Groups that were queueing for their turn. We accordingly set course for Liverpool, and in so doing said farewell to deep-water hunting.

From now until the end of the war in Europe we were engaged in the Battle of the Coastal Waters. From the U-boat point of view, the chief reason why they had operated away from land had been the virtual certainty of being spotted by something, most probably an aircraft, each time they surfaced to charge their batteries. With the Snorchel this was unnecessary, and, when they got used to the thing, boats were able to go literally for weeks on end without surfacing at all. In these circumstances coastal water offered good inducements in the shape of plenty of targets with little extra danger once the minefields in the approaches had been passed. Submarines, it is true, prefer deep to shallow water for ease of manoeuvre, but, to set against that, in shallow water the bottom is conveniently close at hand if the tide is foul, or if they want to lie doggo.

From our point of view shallow water is the devil. I have said a little about 'non-sub' echoes on the asdic; in the waters of the Atlantic you can at least rule out those that come from the bottom, for that is a couple of miles away. It is also not possible for a ' U-boat to bottom in any great depth, and so she must keep moving as long as she is submerged. In shallow water, on the other hand, a U-boat, finding herself in danger of being chased, can take a look at the chart and go to ground among a lot of boulders or in a valley in the sea bed, leaving us the task of combing the bottom and deciding which of the knobs are boulders, or old wrecks, and which may conceivably be the enemy. Add the complication of manoeuvring to get over the top of, or even to remain in contact with, a small bump on the bottom while a tidal stream relentlessly sweeps the ship away, and it can be appreciated that this sort of search calls for the exercise of much faith and patience.

We had to scrap all our hunting methods and think up new ones. At first there was not much success, and several U-boats escaped. Although the number of merchant ships sunk was not really great, the fact that they were sinking off Holyhead or the Eddystone sounded worse than if they had been out in the open sea. Then after a bit the situation began to improve again; the toll of U-boats mounted, and the number of merchant-ship sinkings dropped right away almost to nothing. We had new weapons and devices, but I really think it was more through pegging away and pooling our experiences, helped in no small measure by the School of Tactical Wrens in Liverpool, that we got a pretty good answer to the problem.

The Group changed its composition a great deal during these months, and when the redistribution of ships for the Japanese war began towards the end of 1944 the *Starling* and *Wren* departed, leaving only the *Wild Goose* of the original team to lead the Group. After the last reshuffle we consisted, besides the *Wild Goose*, of the *Loch Fada*, *Loch Ruthven*, *Dominica*, *Labuan* and *Tobago*, all of them frigates. In appearance we had changed greatly, but the Group spirit never flickered, much less failed. It was a fine thing to feel the confidence which our new-comers brought to their work as soon as they were full members of the team. We were the Second Support Group, and were lucky. Other groups flogged the ocean every bit as hard, but never found the chance to show what they could do. Our Group never went really long without a fight, and when that came we were expected to show results, whatever were the names of the ships taking part.

We had one more purple patch in the middle of this campaign of patience and perseverance. It started when we were sharing with another Group in the support of two convoys, one a coastal and the other an ocean convoy. The two convoys were not many miles apart, near the Lizard, when a U-boat torpedoed a small collier at the rear of the coastal convoy. If he had any thought of an uninterrupted retreat after this shot, he had chosen his moment badly, for we all saw it happen and bedlam was let loose. It was organised bedlam, for we were none of us new to the game, but the row was terrific. Every contact that even resembled a submarine was attacked, and the sea was soon strewn with dead fish and bits of flotsam from old wrecks. But one of these chance shots, sounding no better than the rest, was the U-boat. The *Loch Fada* attacked it, and five minutes later a large air bubble broke surface, in the middle of which were five Germans.

The strange thing was that the contact, which was never much good, disappeared altogether, and we looked around the spot off and on for over a week without finding another sign. The survivors said that the U-boat had split open and was filling rapidly when they escaped from the conning-tower, yet there was no trace of oil or debris on the surface. The fear began to grow that the U-boat herself had not been badly hurt, but had crept away with only her conning-tower flooded, which would have been quite possible. Then, on the eighth day, the *Loch Fada*, returning for yet another search, got a fresh bottom contact less than a mile from the buoyed position of the attack and started an oil leak from it. No more evidence could be produced that day, but two days later she returned, found oil still coming up, and split the wreck open to release masses of evidence that this was her U-boat. The survivors' story had been true after all, yet no reason for the complete absence of any evidence of destruction at first has ever been forthcoming.

Meanwhile, in the evening of the day on which that U-boat was sunk, an aircraft reported that she had seen a periscope and some oil only twenty miles away. We broke off our hunt and made our way to the spot as fast as we could, although we could not get there till after dark. There was an unusual number of "non-subs' about, so much so that at one time no less than four of the five ships present were simultaneously investigating different contacts, while a harassed Senior Officer in the fifth ship visited them in turn, or asked questions on the R-T and tried to decide whether any of the contacts was what we were looking for. The *Labuan*'s contact was chosen as possible, and she went in with her pattern of charges, after which we had another look at the spot. While doing this I smelt oil and noticed, in the moonlight, an object floating in a pool of it. I went alongside the object and found it to be of the size and shape of an ordinary oil drum, which, I am afraid, led me to some hasty and uncalled-for conclusions about airmen's eyesight and imaginary periscopes.

We went on searching all night, and by 9 a.m. we had got back to somewhere near the starting point, where again we sighted the 'oil drum'. Something moved me to take another look at it in daylight, and this time I saw that it was no ordinary drum but had what looked like a lug at one end. A davit was rigged and the thing hooked and hoisted on board, where we found that the 'lug' was a wheel operating a quick opening door in the end of the 'drum'. A half turn of this wheel and the whole purpose of the thing was revealed: it was the container for a German dinghy, which lay collapsed inside.

This piece of enemy property, we felt, must have come from the *Labuan*'s target of the night before. The navigator supplied the tidal drift since last night's attack, and a welcome oil streak, a mile long, led to the point from which the oil was coming up. Our guess of the contact to attack had been a good one, and a couple more attacks now brought up the additional evidence that the *Labuan* had made a kill.

Our last incident was in a way odder still. It occurred a fortnight later, very soon after we had settled the matter of the *Loch Fada*'s U-boat. The *Loch Ruthven* got a bottom contact, which she and the *Wild Goose* belaboured, producing a large amount of oil, one or two bits and pieces, and eventually a letter addressed to a sailor in a Norwegian U-boat base. So far, so good, but unfortunately we had the report of a hunt that had ended in the destruction of a U-boat, number given, by another Group in this vicinity six months earlier. We looked it up and checked the position: it was within a few hundred yards of ours, and so we concluded that we had been flogging a dead horse. Even the address on our recovered letter did not help, as no number was on it, and so, most reluctantly, we abandoned our claim. The sequel, which came some months after the war, brought us happiness once more, for the German records showed that another U-boat which did not return had been in that position at about that time, and we were officially credited with her destruction.

In March 1945 Their Majesties inspected the *Wild Goose* in Birkenhead docks, when a number of the Group captains were presented, and a tour was made of the ship. With their unfailing graciousness, and to our great delight, both the King and Queen stopped and spoke to the wardroom wine steward, W H Green, who, as the pivot member of the depth-charge reloaders, was fallen-in with his 'party' wearing a nice new Distinguished Service Medal (DSM) ribbon.

The war had still some months to run, but they passed in much the same way, and without adding to our score. VE-day found us in Liverpool preparing to set out afresh, and a humane Commander-in-Chief put off our departure by a day. We did a turn as reception committee for U-boats in the Channel, but the surrender traffic was light in that part of the world, and we had to content ourselves with a view of the Cornish Riviera. Finally, our orders came to return to harbour, and one lovely evening at the end of May we steamed up the Mersey for the last time as a Group. The *Wild Goose*, flying her banner, led the way, and in close order astern came the rest, each with a broom hoisted at the yard-arm. The Second Support Group's career was ended.

As Others Saw Us

NOTE. The airmen of Coastal Command were our comrades in arms and I have been privileged to obtain accounts of some of the Second Support Group actions, as seen through their eyes, with which to round off the tale. The extracts that follow are taken from the Coastal Command Review, which, unfortunately, gives no names of pilots and air crew taking part, but if anyone of them reads this I hope he will recognise how much we valued his company.

This chapter includes as well some enemy versions of the same incidents.

1. AN ENTIRE PACK DESTROYED

ON the morning of July 30th, 1943, the Germans received an emphatic answer to their new U-boat pack tactics. Surface craft co-operated with seven anti-submarine aircraft, six British and one American, to sink all three U-boats of a pack. The story begins shortly before 10.00 hours when patrolling aircraft intercepted a sighting report from Liberator 0/53. In less than half an hour a Sunderland, R/228, was on the scene circling the three surfaced U-boats which were in V formation steering south-west. The arrival of a Ju-88, which forced the Sunderland to jettison his depth-charges and make for cloud, threatened to spoil the battle. Contact, however, was maintained and soon a Catalina arrived and then left again to guide some naval sloops to the scene. Meanwhile, other aircraft had been diverted to the position and shortly before eleven o'clock two Halifaxes, B/502 and S/502, another Sunderland, U/461, and another Liberator, A/19 Squadron, US Army, were all present.

By one of the most extraordinary coincidences of the war, worth mentioning at this point, the U-boat No. U-461, which was the first to be sunk, was killed by the Sunderland U/461, in the captain's first attack on a U-boat.

The attack was opened by Halifax B/502 on the starboard-wing U-boat. The aircraft attacked from the U-boat's port quarter, dropping three bombs that fell about seventy yards over on the starboard beam of the target. No evidence of damage was seen. In making the attack the Halifax had been met with a heavy concentration of flak from all boats, and was hit in the starboard elevator. Fire was returned and bullet splashes straddled the conning-tower. B/502 then set course for base.

The second Halifax S/502, then attacked the same U-boat, dropping single bombs from a greater height. The attack was made from dead astern, and the first bomb fell close to the stern of the target. The damaged U-boat circled slowly to starboard with dark smoke pouring from abaft the conning-tower. Intense flak was experienced during the run-up. The other bombs failed to hit. About fifteen minutes after the first attack the damaged U-boat slowed down, stopped, and began to settle on an even keel. Some forty men were seen abandoning ship. Just as the conning-tower was sinking, with smoke still pouring out, shells splashed near, and the sloops were seen firing about five miles away.

Before this U-boat had been finally disposed of it had been unsuccessfully attacked by the US Liberator A. This aircraft had already made one attempt to get in an attack in company with Sunderland U/461, but neither aircraft could get through the intense flak. The Sunderland then attacked the port-wing U-boat, while the American pressed home another attack on the already damaged starboard-wing boat. After penetrating intense flak he tracked over the U-boat, confirming that smoke was coming from it, but the bomb release was shot away and the attack was abortive.

The Sunderland's attack was an outright kill. The U-boat had been previously attacked ineffectively by Liberator 0/53 and the aircraft was subjected to a very intense barrage of fire from all the U-boats. This gave U/461 his chance. While the enemy gunners were concentrating on 0/53 the Sunderland came in on the port quarter low down and dropped a stick of depth-charges that straddled. Quantities of orange-coloured froth were given off from the bows of the target and as the aircraft came round again about thirty men were seen in the water, near whom a dinghy was dropped.

There is no doubt that this very accurate attack by U/461 was made possible by the fine effort of Liberator 0/53, but in drawing upon itself such heavy fire this aircraft was badly damaged and could not return to base. It was learned later that it had been able to make a successful forced landing in Portugal.

Seeing two of his colleagues thus disposed of in spite of heavy defensive fire, the captain of the third U-boat decided that his only hope was to dive. This did indeed save him from air attack but not from eventual destruction. The sloops were rapidly closing the scene of action, and soon gained contact. Depth-charge attacks were carried out and the third U-boat joined the others on the bottom.

2. A HARD-LUCK STORY

During her first patrol in May, 1944, U-736 had the misfortune to be detected by Liberator C/224. She was proceeding on the surface during the night of May 24/25 when she was illuminated by the Liberator's searchlight. At the same time the aircraft's guns opened fire, to which the U-boat replied until her quadruple 20-mm. guns failed after five rounds. The Liberator then attacked with depth-charges which were seen to hit the water fifty yards astern of the target with no visible damage resulting.

Soon afterwards the Liberator regained contact and once more illuminated the U-boat. Another stick of depth-charges was dropped, but again no results were seen.

However, inside U-736 the results were only too apparent. Both the gyro and the magnetic compasses were smashed, and the wireless equipment was put out of action and there was a rent three feet long in the pressure hull just below the bow torpedo tubes. By using all the bilge pumps the crew succeeded in reducing the level of the water and caulking the rent. When this had been done U-736 was able to continue submerged at about sixty-five feet. A short time before midnight the next night U-736 was met by five minesweepers and escorted into Lorient.

The repairs in the Keroman dry dock at Lorient lasted nearly two and a half months. During this time the quadruple 20-mm. guns were exchanged for a 37-mm. and a Snorchel was fitted. One of the diesel cylinder heads had been cracked and two others, which were defective, had also been replaced. Late in July she began tests in harbour, but on 26th she went aground near the pen where she was berthed. At low tide she lay in about three feet of water with a list of fifty-one degrees. This caused the acid to spill out of the main torpedo batteries and all the oil ran out of the bearings of the motors, which consequently seized up. She was eventually towed back to the pen, where her torpedoes were landed and new ones embarked. New batteries were also recommended, but before they could be supplied U-736 had to leave in a hurry. The damaged batteries were therefore patched up and the U-boat sailed on August 5th. However, her ill-luck held and the following day she was sunk by HMS *Loch Killin*.

3. SIGHTED AND ATTACKED WHILE SUBMERGED

In the afternoon of August 9th, 1944, Liberator C/53 was flying over the Bay of Biscay when the crew sighted an oil slick. The captain turned to investigate and saw that the slick was over a mile long and about thirty feet wide. It appeared to run about north-east and as the Liberator approached on the same heading, some of the crew saw the shape of a U-boat below the surface just ahead of the apex of the oil trace. The captain immediately lost height in a turn and dropped a marker which fell 150 yards in front of the oil. He then attacked from astern up the oil slick and dropped a stick of depth-charges, using the marker as an aiming point. The depth-charges entered the water between the apex of the oil and the marker, dead in line. When the explosion plumes subsided the, apex of the oil was in the residue of the explosions. As the plumes subsided the rear gunner saw big green bubbles in the middle of the disturbance and a few seconds later other members of the crew saw a profusion of bubbles in the same spot. Ten minutes later oil came to the surface and began to spread out. Half an hour after the attack, when the Liberator flew away to fetch ships of the Second Support Group, the bubbles and oil still persisted. When the ships as well as two Sunderlands had reached the area the Liberator resumed her patrol. The scene was revisited three hours later, when the crew saw quantities of heavy yellow-coloured grease amongst the oil, which was still triangular in shape but had grown very much bigger. The ships were still there and they told the Liberator captain that the oil was increasing and that they had found what looked like bits of U-boat planking. The Liberator then returned to base.

Prisoner-of-War Story. U-608 left Lorient at 2130 hours on August 7th, in company with two other boats. She carried supplies for fourteen weeks. When four miles from Port Louis she dived and proceeded submerged on 8th and 9th. At about 1400 hours on 9th, Liberator C/53 attacked her. A depth-charge exploded forward of the conning-tower and caused damage. She therefore bottomed. Some eight hours later HM ships *Wren* and *Loch Killin* obtained contact and HMS *Wren* dropped a pattern of depth-charges that went off on the bottom very close to the U-boat. Water entered aft and by the torpedo tubes and the lights went out. Everything in the wireless cabinet was smashed and the diesels were torn from their foundations. Eventually the order was given to blow tanks and U-608 surfaced. No ships were in sight, but the batteries were finished and the boat was full of water. Ten minutes later the ship's company abandoned their U-boat, which sank in three minutes. The whole complement of fifty-one was picked up at about 0300 hours on August 10th by HM ships *Wren* and *Loch Killin*.

4. A MOONLIGHT ATTACK

At 0235 hours on August 11th, 1944, Sunderland P/461 (RAAF) was flying over the Bay of Biscay in calm weather and bright moonlight when a contact was picked up fine on the port bow. The captain held on his course until, at five miles' range, he sighted his contact, a fully surfaced U-boat, in the moon-path and broad on the bow. She appeared to be a normal 500-tonner, mounting a big gun forward of the conning-tower, and was steering south-west at about eight knots. The Sunderland turned away until the range had opened to eight miles and then turned back again, holding the contact throughout these manoeuvres. The captain then made a series of S turns to get the U-boat in the moon-path, eventually sighting her again at a range of six miles. At four miles he lost height and at two miles he dived to attack, releasing a stick of depth-charges. He used no illuminant, as he could see the target up-moon in perfect visibility. The depth-charges were dropped across the U-boat's beam, and are stated to have straddled her amidships. The explosion plumes completely obliterated the target. Immediately before the attack the U-boat fired a few shots and what may have been a red recognition cartridge. At the moment of the explosions a bluish-white flash was seen on the U-boat. After the plumes had subsided she was still on the surface, but was stationary. The Sunderland turned to port after the attack and flew past the enemy's stern at a range of 1,000 yards. The German gunners opened up with about six guns, but their fire, though fairly heavy, was most inaccurate. At two miles' range the U-boat disappeared from view and the Sunderland flew off to make contact with the Second Support Group, which was nine miles to the south-east of the position of the attack, and led the ships back to the area. On return to the marker the crew found a patch of oil a hundred feet wide. Searching around, they picked up a contact on the U-boat's original track about two miles ahead of her last position and after three attempts this was illuminated and identified as a radar decoy balloon. The Sunderland reported the position to the ships and continued to stand by. About two and a half hours after the attack a fresh contact was picked up, but it disappeared before anything could be sighted, although it, too, was reported to the ships, who carried out a sweep towards it, and a bit later they informed the Sunderland that they had found an empty dinghy. After having stayed in the area for three and a half hours the Sunderland reached PLE and set course for base.

At 0636 hours on August 12th the U-boat surfaced 3,000 yards ahead of the *Starling* and was heavily engaged and hit by gunfire. She sank five minutes later.

Prisoner-of-War Story. This U-boat, U-385; left St Nazaire on August 9th to try to make La Pallice. On 11th, after proceeding submerged for about twenty hours, the commanding officer decided to use the Snorchel. According to the prisoners it had never worked, and on this occasion, as usual, the boat began to fill with exhaust fumes. The ship's company stuck it as long as they could, but after the commanding officer had passed out, the boat surfaced to ventilate. While she was doing this, Sunderland P/461 attacked. Most of the depth-charges overshot on the starboard quarter, but two did a great deal of damage. The starboard after hydroplane and the rudder were torn off and the starboard screw was put out of action. In addition the outer cap of No. 5 torpedo tube was blown in and the washer on the inside of the cap was blown off; this caused a serious leak. The boat dived, but the air was by no means pure. It was necessary to pump a great deal, and the batteries were very low as it had not been possible to put a charge on during the time the Snorchel was being used.

By 0600 hours on the 12th the air in the boat was so foul that something had to be done. The commanding officer wished to make a run for port, but steering had become almost impossible. He therefore had to surface, although he knew that there were two ships hunting him. To his surprise there were five. These ships opened fire and scored hits forward and aft of the conning-tower, which caused a further entry of water and a short on the armature of the only serviceable motor. The order was then given to abandon ship.

5. U-BOAT KILLED BY AUSTRALIANS

On August 1st, 1943, Sunderland B/10 (RAAF) was on patrol over the Bay of Biscay, flying just beneath cloud base over a heavy sea with the visibility about seven miles. Shortly after 1630 hours the aircraft sighted the Second Support Group and a Catalina engaged in a U-boat hunt. The captain altered course towards them and sighted a U-boat two miles away on the starboard bow. The enemy vessel was about six miles away from the Group and was steering away from them at about ten knots. She carried one big gun forward, one 20-mm. on the bridge and two 20-mm. on the single bandstand. The Sunderland flew over the U-boat and made a tight turn to attack from the U-boat's starboard quarter at sixty degrees to her track. During the approach the front gunner opened fire, but the aircraft was subjected to very accurate return fire from the 20-mm. gun on the bridge. First the Sunderland's inner engine was hit, and then, when the aircraft was about 400 yards away, a hit in the starboard main fuel tank caused petrol to pour out on the bridge. It is believed that all three pilots were wounded. The attack was, nevertheless, gallantly pressed home and a stick of depth-charges was released from close over the top of the U-boat. Charges fell on either side of the target, and the rear gunner saw the U-boat lift out of the water and then sink by the bows. After the attack the Sunderland maintained course for about six miles, turned 180 degrees to port and ditched down-wind at about forty-five degrees to the swell. Apparently the captain was trying to get as near as possible to the ships. The aircraft bounced twice and then settled with the hull very seriously damaged. Six members of the crew succeeded in getting out on the starboard mainplane, which had broken away from the rest of the aircraft. They used this as a raft for about half an hour, and were then picked up by HMS *Wren*, which then proceeded to help the rest of the Group to pick up fourteen survivors from the U-boat.

6. A DIARY FROM THE BAY (CF. PP. 72–76)

Impressions of an officer of the Royal Air Force who was on board HMS Woodpecker during the Second Support Group's operations in the Bay of Biscay

Friday, July 30th

Went on the bridge at midnight. Left the bridge at 4 a.m. and had a few hours' sleep. About 8.30 a.m. the fun really started. What a terrific day. A Sunderland and a Catalina were around and they signalled that no less than three U-boats were on the surface about ten miles away ahead. The SNO in the *Kite* made the signal: 'General Chase.' Off we went at full speed, line abreast… a grand sight… smooth blue sea and blue sky… all ratings and officers at action stations. Soon we saw the aircraft circling low and diving to drop depth-charges. Two of the U-boats were visible by this time and the Sunderland dropped a couple of depth-charges plumb on either side of the conning-tower of one of them. That broke the U-boat's back and he disappeared pretty quickly, leaving some survivors and a raft in the water. Simultaneously, all our ships had opened fire with 4-inch on the second U-boat. He, too, left survivors who had to wait until U-boat No. 3 had been located and dealt with. Not unnaturally, No. 3 dived in some haste and we were now set the task of finding him beneath the surface. It was like great cats stalking an oversize mouse. *Kite* found him first and dropped a pattern of depth-charges. Then *Woodpecker* set about him and dropped depth-charges. *Kite* got a 'fix' and with his direction we proceeded to lay a 'plaster', which is rather what the name denotes. *Wild Goose* repeated the dose, but while she was doing so the first patches of oil were observed and soon it was coming up in great quantities… the sea stank of it. Wood and other wreckage came up too. This was about 3.30 p.m. We recovered various things. *Wren* found some German clothing. The evidence was decisive and the ships (which had been shielding one another during the action) re-formed and made off to pick up survivors. The C-in-C Plymouth signalled 'Well done'; the C-in-C Western Approaches sent 'Warmest congratulations.'

Now for the survivors. We picked up seventeen, including the captain and first officer. The other ships picked up a further fifty or so altogether. Ours were in or clinging to a rubber float, shaped like a big rubber ring. Some were injured. One had a bullet in his stomach and a broken ankle. They were mostly shaking with cold and/or reaction from their experience. Several of them were truculent. Some had never been in a U-boat before… possibly never to sea before. Their life-belts and equipment are excellent. Other survivors are reported some miles away. We are making for them.

Later

Prisoners have been disposed of and are reported happy. Two of our officers have to give up their bunks for the U-boat officers (International Law!). Two in the sick bay look rather mouldy.

The dinghy with six people has just been picked up. They were Huns and not RAF. They had a sail up. One report says that No. 2 submarine contained an RAF officer who had been shot down and picked up by the U-boat. If so, he went down with the U-boat.

Sunday, August 1st

Rather a rough night. Difficult to remain upright in the cabin and shaving is rather tricky. Up on the bridge there is a strong breeze. She is rolling 25–30 degrees. Sheets of spray coming over bridge and captain wraps a towel (my towel… my only towel!) round his neck after being deluged with water. *Woodpecker's* bow keeps on hitting the sea with a hell of a thump, and in the forward cabin it sounds as though tanks were bouncing about on the keel.

U-boat reported at periscope depth some distance away. We alter course and pack on full speed ahead. Things are warming up and we forego lunch and have a sandwich on the bridge. Catalina signals 'No more endurance. Good hunting. Cheerio.' However, two Sunderlands are around and as we approach we can see smoke floats and one of the Sunderlands is evidently going to attack. She dives low and drops depth-charges. Immediately after the attack she is in difficulties. She hits the water and there is an appalling explosion and we just catch sight of the Sunderland's tail before it sinks under the waves. No survivors from that, says the captain, and we shake our heads sadly. Then someone shouts, 'There's a dinghy!' and sure enough some have managed to get away. *Wren*, being nearest, collects them. They are six in number and some of them injured. The story goes that both pilots were killed by gunfire. The engines and fuel tanks were shot up by the U-boat. But the important thing is that they sank the U-boat. No doubt about that, because our sister ships picked up about twenty Huns.

We now have about a hundred Germans on the five ships as another contingent was picked up last night.

Monday, Bank Holiday, August 2nd.

Another U-boat sunk by RAF but not in our range of vision. Ship has quite a nasty roll. When having breakfast I went clean over backwards in my chair, but didn't get hurt… much.

Some abortive U-boat contacts were pursued during the morning. After lunch the alarm bells sounded. Arrived on the bridge at the double and found things going on apace. The captain whispered in my ear, 'We have had a signal from a spotting aircraft saying that four Narvik destroyers are twelve miles away making converging course on us.'

R. figured that if two of our five ships got home at all we should be lucky. C-in-C Plymouth signalled happily that he didn't think that they were quite as big as Narviks and that the cruiser would .be there tomorrow! Their masts were sighted half an hour later!

The U-boat prisoners weren't so happy either, they didn't like going down in the hold.

We continued to steer towards the enemy in order to close the range and the tension remained and speculation was rife. Four masts are sighted on the horizon, soon to be identified as another escort group. They aren't much good as surface-fighting ships, but anyhow they are friends, not foes. Reports about the enemy are coming in again. He is changing course away from us. We alter to intercept him, but he has superior speed. Two oldish destroyers have also come into the picture and although they go flat out, the Gerries for some reason are running for home like scalded cats. As the light begins to fade we form into a most extraordinary contingent with the destroyers on our port and the others to starboard. The captain is rampaging about it. Says we are over the ocean like a lot of blue-bottomed flies and if somebody doesn't collide with someone else during the night he will be in no ordinary way surprised. What a Bank Holiday!

Tuesday, August 3rd

There has been plenty of aircraft activity today and our support has arrived. A cruiser and two destroyers came up at thirty knots through our line, turned around like guardsmen and away again. Nice to see them all the same.

Wednesday, August 4th

We have turned for home and expect to arrive on Friday. We have done nearly 4,000 miles (sea miles) and it will be well over 4,300 by the time we get back.

Thursday, August 5th

Had a good night in spite of being shot out of bunk. We have had a gale warning and the ships are rolling good and plenty.

Life is unbearably unpleasant in the cabin. One is shot from one wall to the other: everything movable moves rapidly all over the place… chairs, books, barograph, drawers, food. We have just tried to have lunch, but it's an almost impossible feat. Every now and again the bunk tilts forty-five degrees and off we slide to the opposite wall again.

We are somewhere off the Scilly Isles. I hope somebody knows where we really are. It's dark and still very rough.

Friday, August 6th

All calm again. Line ahead. Just making the Eddystone Lighthouse. Off old uniforms, flannel trousers, golf jackets, etc., and on with pure white collars and best uniforms. Through the boom. Dress the ships perfectly. In the distance is Plymouth Hoe. Yeoman of signals, peering through his telescope, says signal by C-in-C is 'Well done'.

C-in-C himself takes the salute and the sight of those five fine ships entering the harbour and passing the saluting base with the leading ship playing 'A-Hunting We Will Go' on her loud-hailers is a thing I will never forget.

SECOND SUPPORT GROUP U-BOAT RECORD

HM Sloops

Starling	*Wild Goose*	*Wren*
Kite	*Woodpecker*	*Magpie*
Whimbrel		*Woodcock*

HM Frigates

Loch Fada	*Loch Killin*	*Lochy*
Loch Ruthven	*Dominica*	*Labuan*
	Tobago	

No.	Date	Ships taking part	Ship Which	
			First Detected	Destroyed
1 U–202	1/2.6.43	Starling, Woodpecker, Kite, Wild Goose, Wren	Starling	Starling Gunfire
2 U–119	24.6.43	Starling, Woodpecker, Kite, Wren, Wild Goose	Starling	Starling
3 U–449	24.6.43	Wren, Woodpecker, Kite, Wild Goose, Starling (damaged)	Wren	Group depth-charges
4 U–462	30.7.43	Kite, Woodpecker, Wren Wild Goose, Woodcock	Aircraft	Group gunfire Aircraft S/502 Squadron
5 U–504	30.7.43	Kite, Wren, Woodpecker, Wild Goose, Woodcock	Wren Kite	Wild Goose
6 U–226	6.11.43	Starling, Kite, Woodcock	Kite	Woodcock

No.	Date	Ships taking part	Ship which	
			First Detected	Destroyed
7 U-842	6.11.43	Starling, Wild Goose, Magpie	Wild Goose	Wild Goose
8 U-592	31.1.44	Starling, Wild Goose, Magpie (Screening - Woodpecker, Wren, Kite)	Wild Goose	Wild Goose Starling
9 U-762	9.2.44	Wild Goose, Woodpecker (Rest as in No.8 Screening)	Wild Goose	Woodpecker
10 U-734	9.2.44	Wild Goose, Starling	Wild Goose	Wild Goose Starling
11 U-238	9.2.44	Starling, Kite, Magpie	Kite	Magpie
12 U-424	11.2.44	Wild Goose, Woodpecker	Wild Goose	Wild Goose

No.	Date	Ships taking part	Ship Which	
			First Detected	Destroyed
13 U-263	19.2.44	*Woodpecker, Starling*	*Woodpecker*	*Woodpecker* *Starling*
14 U-653	15.3.44	*Wild Goose, Starling*	*Wild Goose* Aircraft A/825 Sqdn. from HMS *Vindex*	*Starling*
15 U-961	30.3.44	*Starling*	*Starling*	*Starling*
16 U-473	5.5.44	*Wild Goose, Wren, Starling*	*Wild Goose*	All
17 U-333	31.7.44	*Starling, Wren, Loch Killin, Loch Fada* *Lochy, Dominica*	*Loch Killin*	*Loch Killin* *Starling*
18 U-736	6.8.44	*Starling, Wren, Loch Killin, Loch Fada* *Lochy, Dominica*	*Loch Killin*	*Loch Killin*

No.	Date	Ships taking part	First Detected	Destroyed
			Ship Which	
19 U-608	9.8.44	Wren, Loch Killin, Starling, Loch Fada Dominica	Aircraft C/53 Squadron	Wren
20 U-385	11.8.44	Starling, Wren, Loch Fada, Loch Killin, Dominica	Group and Aircraft P/461 Sqd.	Group gunfire
21 U-1018	27.2.45	Wild Goose, Loch Fada, Loch Ruthven Dominica, Labuan	Loch Fada	Loch Fada
22 U-327	27.2.45	Loch Fada, Wild goose, Loch Ruthven, Dominica, Labuan	Loch Fada Aircraft H/112 Sqdn. (US)	Labuan Loch Fada
23 U-683	12.3.45	Loch Ruthven, Wild Goose	Loch Ruthven	Loch Ruthven